Ryan

The Power Play

A tragicomedy in five acts

London 0208 834 0500.
★ Hammersmith

Duckpaddle Publishing

Ryan J-W Smith

𝕿𝖍𝖊 𝕻𝖔𝖜𝖊𝖗 𝕻𝖑𝖆𝖞 ©

Copyright © 2003 Ryan J-W Smith

First published in 2003 by Duckpaddle Publishing

Printed and bound in Great Britain by
Duffield Printers Ltd, 421 Kirkstall Road, Leeds.

ISBN 0-9515956-3-6

Amateur and Professional Performing Rights: applications for performance in excerpt or in full, by non-professionals or professionals in any medium or in any language throughout the world should be addressed to -

Duckpaddle Publishing
P.O. Box 147, Dewsbury,
WF12 0WZ, U.K.
fax: +44 (0) 1924 485898

No performance of any kind may take place unless a licence has been obtained. Application should be made before rehearsals begin.

www.ryanjwsmith.com

That we be forsaken they would convince;
For those who have fallen, here be your Prince.

The Power Play

or

Prince Valentino

for Jean

Dramatis Personae

RUFUS, King of Florence.

ISOBEL, Queen of Florence.

VALENTINO, Prince of Florence.

JAQUES, Valentino's manservant.

DON GRENALDO, half-brother to the King.

MARCELLO, Don Grenaldo's son, a soldier.

PHOEBE, Don Grenaldo's daughter, a maid.

LADY MARIA, Valentino's lover.

BARTHES, Lady Maria's manservant.

JEZEBEL, a courtesan.

OFFICER, of the King's court.

FRIAR LAWRENCE.

Guards and Attendants.

Scene: Florence, Italy.

I.1 *Enter Jaques and Barthes.*
JAQUES. Freedom, Barthes, 'tis all the rage these days;
Freedom of mind, of spirit and morals.
'Tis even so writ in various plays,
Though wordsmiths these days rest on loose laurels.
But not my master, Prince Valentino,
He'd do well to lie a whole night with a
Maid or Lady, whom e'er he deflowers;
By morning he's always well out of sight.
Sneaking home in the cold early hours,
10 Waking me up to recant his triumph,
I pour the tea, he talks like a giant:
In shock she'll awaken; alone, apart,
Searching the mansion for sign of her Prince,
Yet all she will find is a broken heart,
The echoes of passion passed long time since!
As for thy Mistress, Lady Maria,
I doubt he has further plans past tonight.
Say you she came here to tame my sire?
'Tis easier cultivate dark to light!
20 BARTHES. Yet promised he her to take in the church,
To have and to hold and that sort of thing.
JAQUES. I swear, Barthes, she's been left in the lurch;
Sweetest delights hide the bitterest sting.
BARTHES. But she is a Lady and he a Prince!
How could he do it? Jaques, tell me why?
JAQUES. Look, if I had my way his eyes I'd rinse
With the strongest soap that money could buy.
I'd force him view the sharp pain he unrests,
The heart-ache and longing, the loss and grief.
30 But all he sees are sieges and conquests;
He's a cherry stealer, a petty thief!
BARTHES. I cannot this fathom.
JAQUES.   You think you're the first?
'Twix him and the Devil, my master is worse!
There's nought he'll not do in parting their thighs:
Proclamations, swearing, notes, heavy sighs,
Presents, surprises, a weekend for two,
That trip up the Eiffel Tower was new!
Yet in the end it boils down to one thing,
Once he has plucked 'em, he needs a new fling.
40 BARTHES. Yet doth he not fear the wrath of Heaven?

He's not so young now, passed twenty-seven!
JAQUES. He cares nothing for God, manners, or grace;
Ask him the time and he'd spit in your face!
He's a dog carved in the shape of a man;
Atheist, Judas, the spawn of Satan!
BARTHES. Here he comes.
JAQUES.   Holy Christ! Don't say a word;
Whatever you know was not from me heard!
If thou speakest ought of what I here cried,
I shall but deny it; I'll say thou lied!
Enter Valentino, Jaques hugs him.
50   O good, my sweet Prince! How much I thee missed!
VALENTINO. Too much, it would seem. Come, chew on my fist!
          Valentino swings at Jaques, he ducks.
JAQUES. Thanks, your Lordship, I've already eaten.
VALENTINO. Never be clever, I'll see thee beaten.
          Another swing at Jaques, he ducks.
BARTHES. Forgive me, sir, but Lady Maria?
VALENTINO. Is bound to follow, as smoke by fire.
LADY MARIA. *(off)* Come thee hither thou adulterous swine!
VALENTINO. Jaques, tonight we'll take super at nine.
Enter Maria.
MARIA. Impudent dealer, wherefore art thou so;
What manner of breeding derived thee thus?
60   To be so dark, so foul with swift cunning;
What man measures life by the hearts he is
Winning? Treacherous cur, a pox on thy parts!
Thy touch is ill-fated, it beckons my soul
With thoughts of desire and lusting untold.
Sweet charms thou hadst to combine with attire,
Even the elements did themselves conspire
To present this man as both darkness and light;
I swear, I've never seen evil so bright!
A Prince indeed, yet only in title,
70   For you'll never match poor loves requital.
Thine eyes, my Lord, match not thy sweet smile,
For they are the devil's and you his child!
Yet with all that I hate thee, I love thee still;
O heaven help me, I must be quite ill!
You say nothing? Mark, Valentino is dumb!
Whilst this Lady dies do you bite your thumb?
Am I not virtue, yet am I not fair;

Is Maria not true, does she not care?
Then truthfully speak to the aching heart
80   Thy averous nature so tore apart,
For should thee fail to conquer my charge,
Feline vexation will certain enlarge.
VALENTINO. Maria, my sweet, in truth I confess
I loved thee so much my heart did protest!
Would the stars in heaven refuse to shine
Thy light would guide me, our harbour to find.
Such visions as these consumed my poor brain,
Increased jealous nature, causing me pain.
Whence without you I was, at your own behest,
90   Thy image did haunt me with heaves of unrest.
Mine only defence 'gainst a heart attacked
Was distracting mine eye, thus to retract.
I was with another, 'tis as you suspect,
And then with her sister, just out of respect,
Yet both were cipher, of nothing to thee.
JAQUES. *(To Barthes)* He had them together, dinner for three!
VALENTINO. Moreover; I swear, I am not at fault,
Though I see you dispute with clear revolt,
Yet 'twas thy crime, my love, I bear no shame,
100   Carry no crosses, nor shoulder the blame;
'Twas thee insisted thou needeth more time
To commit thy heart before loving mine.
MARIA. But -
VALENTINO. Perhaps 'tis just I love thee more true!
I am for thee as a horse is to glue:
(Kneeling) Condemned, enslaved, shackled, forlorn! I could
Not alone fight the time and scorn!
BARTHES. *(Aside)*   Good God!
VALENTINO. So pity me love, 'twas thee I did miss;
Rekindle my soul and give us a kiss!
MARIA. O my true love!
VALENTINO.   My sweet dove!
      They kiss passionately
BARTHES.   Lord above!
110   This is beyond the good sense of reason.
JAQUES. To not love the Prince of Florence is treason.
BARTHES. A model for lust in manner and gait.
JAQUES. He dines every night, yet keeps a full plate!
BARTHES. He holds all women, yet keeps them at bay.

JAQUES. There's plenty love a good roll in the hay!

BARTHES. His eye doth confuse them.

JAQUES.   His tongue doth arouse.

BARTHES. They say he's a big one.

JAQUES.   For pleasing the crowds!

MARIA. O no, my dear Lord, I beg thee refrain,

For have we an audience, I see it plain.

120 VALENTINO. Aye, Jaques! Why, thou knowest Maria?

JAQUES. Not quite as you do, but yes, my sire.

MARIA. Meet me tonight, my Prince, my sweet heaven!

VALENTINO. I'll come from behind my castle at seven.

Leave now thy servant, Barthes, in my charge,

'Til we meet us tonight, thence to discharge.

MARIA. Should thee wish, my love, I'll too be mastered.

BARTHES. *(Aside)* Can you believe it?

JAQUES. *(Aside)*   He's such a bastard!

MARIA. *Au revoir, mon amour.*

VALENTINO.   *À plus tard, ma chérie.*

                                        Exit Maria.

JAQUES. My too cunning master, how is't with thee?

130 VALENTINO. Well, my sad servant, as well you can see.

I'm in health, Jaques, the rash has healed!

JAQUES. *(To Barthes)* Hatless he went when ploughing some field.

VALENTINO. 'Twas not the earth, but the sea I was fishing;

Know not her stock, you'd best stick to kissing.

Come, we must venture again to the town

To visit close friends who'll worship my crown.

JAQUES. You mean Polly Peech, the three penny whore?

VALENTINO. Ne'er speak that way of a girl I adore!

        Valentino swings at Jaques, he ducks. Another swing, contact.

BARTHES. I fear we cannot.

VALENTINO.   What!?

BARTHES.   Thy father, the King,

140 Who doth so detest thy base fornicating,

Hath summoned thyself by royal decree

To join him at court. Aye, himself and thee.

VALENTINO. What would he with us, we have no quarrel?

BARTHES. Methinks his discomfort may be moral.

VALENTINO. Well, have ye no fear, his mind I foresee;

I'll charm and appease, then dinner's on me.

Come let us drudge unto his grave estate,

Ere drinking and lust shall be our main plate.

                        Exit Valentino and Barthes.

JAQUES. See what I mean, a Prince without scruples;
150   He is the master and all be his pupils!
Exeunt.

I.2   *Enter the King, Queen, Grenaldo, Phoebe, Guards and Attendants.*
RUFUS. Brother Grenaldo! Wherefore attend we
The will of our issue; are we not King?
GRENALDO. But of course, dear brother.
RUFUS.   Be this not the
Royal ring?
GRENALDO. So it is, your Majesty.
RUFUS. Be this wattle and daub not mine palace?
GRENALDO. O 'tis must assuredly thine, my Liege.
RUFUS. Then present our son to sooth swift malice.
GRENALDO. A half-brother's love is double with us;
Which being so, I shall trace thy son thus.
Exit Grenaldo.

10   RUFUS. Fair niece, Phoebe, bring us water and wine;
Our noble Queen shall pass fair this ill time.
PHEOBE. Aye, my Lord.
Exit Phoebe.

RUFUS. *(Aside)* Had she two, we'd displace Valentino
To a desolate shore, an island cell
And render him love-sick like Orsino,
Then banish his choice; in pain he needs dwell.
To strip him of title, monies and wealth,
Replacing with virtue, manners and health.
Was there ever a Prince pretty as he
20   In charms, in grace and in fortune tax free?
Yet to what fine art doth he ploy his visage?
'Tis for Polly, Anne, for clandestine massage!
And of his sharp wit, his language and art?
'Tis for lying, cheating their thighs apart!
A man must savour his youth, 'tis assured,
Yet by thirty methought he'd be allured
To waifs of beauty, there's plenty about,
Wherefore will his heart not quarrel or shout
'Gainst his nature to ruin every daughter?
30   He needs break hearts like rivers need water.
We are not in our prime, 'tis fair to say,
So the crown needs an heir without delay.
The Prince shall wed, the King shall have his way;
Thus, to re-course, we stage the power play.

11

> For should we chance die and Valentino
> Be not married, our precious line would cease
> To run when his petty part is carried.

Enter Valentino, Jaques, Barthes, Phoebe and Don Grenaldo.

> GRENALDO. Prince Valentino of Florence, my Lord.
> VALENTINO. Uncle Grenaldo, is that a new sword?
40 Father, you're alive! What news, art thou well?
> And mother, how goes it in thy tight cell?
> RUFUS. Tardy and offensive; we're not best pleased
> In thy 'haviour of present, pray conceal
> Thee thy spite; let thy manner be pleasant.
> VALENTINO. I am but thy humble servant, my Lord;
> What e're thy will be, I shall here record.
> How couldst I do else? You're gentle and kind,
> So quiet in nature and out of your mind!
> RUFUS. Peace!
> VALENTINO. What's this, my King, be something amiss?
50 Do my mere playful jibes threaten thy bliss?
> RUFUS. Break not another word from thy false lips;
> Have we our fill of thy insipid quips!
> ISOBEL. Sweet Valentino, for my sake be calm,
> For others bear the scorn of thy salt charm.
> VALENTINO. For thee, dear mother, I shall grow manners,
> Though my heart beats cold to others' clamours.
> RUFUS. Valentino, my Prince, our only son,
> Thy unregenerate countenance starts
> And we fear thy wit's undone. We know not
60 Wherefore you quibble in this ill-manner,
> Nor wherein thy entertainment is sought
> In seeking out our violent stammer,
> Yet have we done with reasonèd questions.
> Thy prurience hath led thy soul astray,
> Where we find thee armed to disobey
> Our smallest order, our kindest request.
> Nay, you probe our office, every word a test
> Of patience, loyalty and most of blood!
> No more shall we endure this torrential
70 Flood of insolent, unmannerly discord.
> Thou art a rudesby! A shallow fellow
> Full of deep facets, yet not so mellow
> As raging winds or electrical storms!
> A gut full of spleen set on to mourn our

12

Passing with each new breath. 'Pon this issue
Have we considered counsel and would thee
Heed our tune. Take stock of thy position:
Has Valentino wealth? Possess he health?
Doth he all that sweet fortune could bestow
80   Sans the scars of dreams without fruition?
Thy boyhood is spent, time the man to know.
Yet men cannot breed by themselves alone,
Another is needed, as the butcher
Wields the knife, so sharpen thy wits and get
Thee a wife!
VALENTINO. Ha, ha, ha, ha, ha, ha, ha!
RUFUS. You laugh? But, of course, 'tis as expected,
Yet know this, our will shall be respected!
VALENTINO. O how you do twerp, fat sparrow, poor lark;
To twitter from dawn to sleepiest dark!
90   *A wife for the Prince, a marriage indeed;*
Nay, do as I say and follow my lead!
I had rather consign to the devil
Than bind to one or sink to thy level!
RUFUS. You shall be married and in but three days
The churches and citizens shall sing thy praise,
For should you refuse to ply with this act
We shall disinherit and thy title retract.
VALENTINO. Thou liest; thou hast not the stomach for this.
RUFUS. Have I the stomach and the meat withal;
100   What needs a man fear when heeding his call?
Thou art lost to me like tears in the rain,
What more harm then should I lose thee again?
The heavens may open, the sun may shine,
Thou shalt be married or erased from time.
We'll no longer endure, no more support
Thy bedroom fanatics, thy midnight sport.
No more bastards shall be issued in Florence!
I tell thee now boy, abstain thy abhorrence.
Go to then, let all jocund be. These, his
Servants, come ye hither with me!
110   BARTHES and JAQUES.   My Lord.
GRENALDO. Come all, away!
ISOBEL. Think well on't, my son, for 'tis not so cruel;
Who plays forever is forever's fool.
                          Exeunt all but Valentino.

VALENTINO. I have thought on't, as much as it deserve,
And find I no reason, why, 'tis absurd
To condemn a Prince perforce to marry
For his father's preservation, nay I'll
Not tarry! These methods are too spongy;
A nefarious plan! Of what great crime
120   Be I guilty, but that I am a man?
'Tis unnatural to lie with but one mate!
As adulterer I'd not hesitate
In act, in thought, in deed, in look; I love
All God's creatures when they bite on my hook!
Howe'er, his rank nature I trust also;
The King will cut me, disown, dishonour,
If provide him I not a grandson so.
That it should come to this, *prendo una donna!*
Methinks there's a dark star shines bright above,
130   Soft whispering fate, so adieu sweet love.
I shall not be my possessive father
Reluctant in mirth and thawed like the dew;
I ne'er bematch my contriving mother,
The victim of lovers, her sheets run through.
Wherefore must I seek the mother of mine
When all I am good for is lusting and wine?
O God! I'll not think upon this notion,
For the mind can free fearful emotion.
Perchance my father should fatal slip take,
140   Swallow some poison by deadly mistake
Or meet a point in the deep city night?
Nay, I'll burn counter, but not snuff his light.

Enter Barthes and Jaques.

How now, fellows, what's his essay for thee?
BARTHES. Charged we two are: make a husband to be!
VALENTINO. Ha! A cuckold means you? I think not so.
Be sure tell my father where he can go!
JAQUES. Then what's to be done, for he'll keep his word?
VALENTINO. Come, let us now speak apart and unheard.
To glut immortal through our lawful kin;
150   I tell thee plain boys, to wed is a sin!

Exeunt.

I.3   *Enter Phoebe and Don Grenaldo.*

GRENALDO. Hear thee, daughter, how the Prince must be wed?
PHEOBE. Aye, my Lord, 'tis all about my poor head.

GRENALDO. Thy brother Marcello's a soldier now,
Bestriding to make his good father proud,
Yet long have I wished great things for Phoebe.
PHEOBE. Wherefore then maketh a servant of me?
GRENALDO. To service others is to know God's will;
Soon all of us sample the humbling pill.
PHEOBE. Yet I have sucked on't and sometime swallowed;
10   T'hath been my whole life I have thee followed.
GRENALDO. Then stick to thy path and obey me now,
For I'd have thee match the Prince and here's how:
Soon shall he quit the palace by this hall,
I have this safe for my servants see all,
Daughter, sweet Phoebe, entice his fair eye,
Engage him in verse if thy brains apply.
Flutter thy eyelids, thy dress passed thy heels
Let thy heart free so excitement it feels.
Keep thine eyes clear, yet then cover thy lips;
20   Enhance thy features, make use thy good bits!
Be vice-ridden bound in a virtuous cloth,
Be the light that attracts the amorous moth,
Be the angel ready to touch hell's fire,
Be the one thing all men truly desire:
That devilish dish that no man can touch,
For once 'tis tasted he craves it too much.
Be enticed aloof, polite, yet unfair
And soon you'll hold him in sweetest despair.
'Tis this bitter place all men long to find,
30   (It exists no-where except in their mind),
Yet you are the key to open this door;
Do not grant his ease and ne'er be his whore!
Instead, a woman, who knows her own worth,
Let man be a man and we shall know mirth.
Do not fall in love, blinded of reason
And judgment of thee shall find new season.
In good time you may grow to fondness sure,
Let this be in passing behind closed doors.
In short, Phoebe, I do say only this,
40   Attract his heart, but ne'er let him thee kiss.
PHEOBE. But love him I have now several years.
GRENALDO. You love him already? My greatest fears
Come upon me now in my shortest shrift.
I pray, of the gab, thou has the sweet gift?

15

PHEOBE. So I have, my Lord, I have been coached well.
GRENALDO. The Prince approaches, alas, we shall tell.
Now play thee true, keep thy action subtle;
Nothing is worse than theatre's rebuttal.
PHEOBE. O true, I agree!
GRENALDO.   Behind the arras
50   Will I hide myself. Child, take care, be
Mysterious deep and we shall know wealth.
Enter Valentino, Barthes and Jaques.
VALENTINO. See you where Signor Grenaldo hath hid?
BARTHES. Very well, my Lord.
VALENTINO.   What say you he would
A Queen for a daughter?
JAQUES.   'Tis apparent,
My Lord.
VALENTINO. Come, let us play; I shall court her!
(Aloud) Why, dear gentle Gods, what vision is this,
Barthes, Jaques, is my reason amiss?
Do I but sleep and so dream of my love
Or doth she appear like Venus above,
60   Infrequently rare, this wonderful sight;
O tell me friends that my sight is all right?
BARTHES. This beauty's real.
JAQUES.   'Tis heaven assured.
VALENTINO. I tell thee now, I am total allured!
O purest of maids, I must thee adore.
PHEOBE. How now, my Lord?
GRENALDO. *(Aside)*   'Tis most wondrous sure!
VALENTINO. I beg thee speak, what cloud brought thee hither?
PHEOBE. 'Twas none, sweet sir, I came by the river.
My father, Grenaldo, works for the King.
VALENTINO. Then you must be Phoebe, a heavenly thing!
70   I pray thee, let me admire the while,
So long have I sought to detail thy smile.
GRENALDO. *(Aside)* O he is caught, he is caught!
PHEOBE.   Very well,
My Lord, as thy servant thou may, yet I
Hope this imbalance might well change someday.
VALENTINO. Thou art a servant, what business it this?
To shackle Aphrodite, we'll speak further
On this.
GRENALDO. *(Aside)* O bliss, this is bliss!

VALENTINO.   But for now,
My kind cousin, I ask but one favour:
The tiniest kiss so might I savour
Elysium here on earth.
80   PHEOBE.   My fair Lord,
I cannot.
GRENALDO. *(Aside)* Goodly child; joy and mirth!
VALENTINO. Thou art a great treasure, 'tis plain to see,
Yet grant this one wish; be precious to me.
PHEOBE. As thy poor maid I may not disagree,
So tenderous be and take me lightly!
          They kiss.
JAQUES. Sweet angels and ministers defend thee!
GRENALDO. *(Aside)* What did he say? What passes? I would see!
VALENTINO. I pray, walk me through this arch just yonder,
For contents within I long to plunder.
                              Exit Valentino and Phoebe.
90   BARTHES. Perchance we should sit and rest ourselves here.
JAQUES. He's usually swift, so we'd best keep near.
BARTHES. Look you, see whereat the Prince hath travelled.
JAQUES. He's stopped in the hall, something unravelled.
BARTHES. How seems the fair maid Phoebe, can you tell?
JAQUES. Her head's at an angle; she's taking it well.
BARTHES. Pray sit thee Jaques, 'tis rudeness to stare.
JAQUES. I don't think her father would like his head there!
Noises off.
BARTHES. What's happening now?
JAQUES.   He's breaking her in.
BARTHES. Such screams of delight!
JAQUES.   Now that is a sin!
100   BARTHES. How long do you think we may have to wait?
JAQUES. The Prince is coming, I can tell by his gait.
Enter Valentino and Phoebe.
VALENTINO. Come, come, dear friends, we must venture at once,
For Phoebe is weak and needs wash her sconce.
          They kiss.
Adieu, ma Chérie, I'll see thee anon,
Follow, good servants, from here we are gone.
                              Exit Valentino, Barthes and Jaques.
Grenaldo comes forth.
GRENALDO. O my sweet child, what is't I have done?
PHEOBE. Bless thee father, I ne'er had so much fun!

GRENALDO. Thither to thine chamber to recompose
Our plans for conquest and fetch thee some clothes!

Exeunt.

I.4   *Enter Lady Maria.*

MARIA. O where is my love, my darling, my Prince?
He touched me this morning and I've not seen
Him since. What could have detained him, for he
Promised me true to crave only my heart,
Our love to renew this hour tonight?
Wherefore is he absent? Doth he mock me
Again? How much more 'till I him refrain?
Yet whom do I fool? For I know too well
Of one love and purgatory he would choose hell!
10   Know I in my soul he does not need me,
Nor doth he desire our wedding to see.
He takes as he wants the flowers of maids
Who offer them gladly; sing to his praise.
Indeed, I sense I'm but one of many,
Yet I'd sooner some than not have any!
And for my hot sins can I only believe
In his devilish eyes that easy deceive,
That soothe all tempers to his perception;
Such bitter delight, such sweet deception!
20   Yet what if I were the tables to turn
To set him up so Maria he'd yearn?
To cut his power I needs must devise
A perilous plot, some nasty surprise.
Perchance I take another hot lover,
To arouse his heart and thus uncover
The jealousy within through my wanton
Fire? From thence my possession is all
He'd aspire. Aye, wherefore should I honour
Rules set by a man? My hunger is great,
30   I shall take all I can! An' he shall pay!
Maria will lie, she'll cheat as you'll see;
If men-folk can do it why cannot we?
But what's that I hear, she's a jade, a tart?
Then rip up my soul and tear out my heart!
'Tis time for men to truly discover
The pain of life with a feckless lover.

Enter Valentino.

VALENTINO. Maria, my sweet, to whom do you speak?

18

MARIA. O no-one, my Prince, 'twas thee I did seek
In the heavens above, for did I call
40   Thy name oft and again, unto my shame.
Yet where is my servant, Barthes, my steed?
VALENTINO. Ah, the King of Barthes himself had need.
'Tis well passed seven, I apologise great.
MARIA. No words, my Prince, let us not hesitate
To a brook or hedge or vale or tree,
I care nought which for I long him to see!
I've held all week for thy puppy's passion,
So take me now in similar fashion!

Maria begins to undress.

VALENTINO. Could not we sit for a moment or two,
50   For I would know somewhat else we might do?
Perchance we could read or look at the sky,
There's many a sonnet I'd like to try?
MARIA. A sonnet, my Lord, a book or the sky?
I do beg your pardon, can I ask why
You speak in this most ridiculous rhyme?
I'll instruct thee cease; do not waste my time!
VALENTINO. I am yet a Prince with rule in this land.
MARIA. This country is held by thy father's firm hand.
VALENTINO. I pray do not mock me within this wise,
60   My inherited anger hath global size.
MARIA. Come, come, my Prince, will you use me or no,
For if you will not I fear I must go.
VALENTINO. Very well, woman, lead on to thy store;
(Aside) Grant me safe passage, my pickle is raw!
                                                    Exeunt

I.5   *Enter Barthes and Jaques.*
BARTHES. How is't that we should the Prince find a wife?
JAQUES. He seems not even to care for his strife!
BARTHES. No sooner do we begin our session -
JAQUES. He rushes off for Maria's lesson.
BARTHES. And but three short nights have we to succeed.
JAQUES. The king will then banish all and at speed.
BARTHES. We have been set a most rough employment.
JAQUES. No God either Highness could make relent.
BARTHES. Let's tackle this with the arms of science.
10   JAQUES. Simple logic may conquer defiance.
BARTHES. Valentino's a man like most others.
JAQUES. Delighting in music and revels so.

19

BARTHES. He drinks.
JAQUES.   He swears.
BARTHES.   Has so many lovers -
JAQUES. That each of his pride he hardly doth know.
BARTHES. Yet this last act is perchance not so sane,
For 'tis unheard of -
JAQUES.   To such an extreme.
His lascivious heart can ne'er refrain
From sordid affairs.
BARTHES.   Existing unclean!
JAQUES. 'Tis all that he thinks on.
BARTHES.   Both night and day.
20   JAQUES. He orates and performs his life away!
BARTHES. Within this issue we'll find our saviour.
JAQUES. His strength and his folly in women lies.
BARTHES. To all things sex is linked his behaviour.
JAQUES. He doth this attract like a compost flies.
BARTHES. Yet deep in his heart beats the tune of love,
Faintly, softly, though to him still unheard.
JAQUES. The pigeon must now transform to a dove
And learn to fly with the purest of birds.
BARTHES. But how to wake the faintest of voices
30   To sing together and so stir his soul?
JAQUES. Let's consider more desperate choices.
BARTHES. Actresses?
JAQUES.   Singers?
BARTHES.   Those dancers on poles?
JAQUES. Someone of his own peculiar notion.
BARTHES. A midnight master.
JAQUES.   A tamer of men.
BARTHES. A girl untouched by female emotion.
JAQUES. The ultimate vixen!
BARTHES.   The dirtiest hen!
JAQUES. The whoremonger's heaven!
BARTHES.   The proud man's hell!
We shall find and convince -
JAQUES and BARTHES.   Sweet Jezebel!
JAQUES. Think you straight he will fall for this hussy,
40   For she is a pro and he's so fussy?
BARTHES. She is the sweetest that I've ever seen;
If nought be his title, she'll be his queen.
JAQUES. The King would behead us if he but knew

The line of men his new daughter went through.
BARTHES. Then we'll refine her, renew and redress,
'Till none can refute, she is the fairest.
JAQUES. 'Tis agreed.
BARTHES.   And most assuredly so.
JAQUES. We shall delicate be.
BARTHES.   And transform us a hoe!
                                  Exeunt

II.1 *Enter the King, Queen, Don Grenaldo, Phoebe.*
RUFUS. Say you he in this manner abused her
Within our lodge and upon her person?
GRENALDO. To that I did hear, I again refer:
The Prince convinced her his life would worsen
If upon her lips he place not a kiss,
To which she agreed, being his servant,
From there he lured her aside and amiss
Whereat, by report, his lust was fervent.
ISOBEL. Yet saw you not the Prince in this action?
10   GRENALDO. Nay, my Lady, though I heard reaction
From my poor daughter as she did protest
Against his plans to undo and undress.
ISOBEL. What say you on this matter, young Phoebe,
Did the Prince mar thee as here it is claimed?
PHEOBE. In sooth, good lady, he was not restrained!
He did mark, caress me, and take his fill,
Yet in all that passed I gave my free will.
GRENALDO. Forgive her prattle, she is yet still ill;
His sin was of such swift dexterity
20   That my poor girl gained his temerity.
RUFUS. Thunderous villain! For this he'll suffer,
By light of this day state justice he'll know!
Our punishing heart will beat e're rougher;
What wouldst thou have for thy pains Grenaldo?
GENALDO. Though much offence was caused in relation
We would not have her revenged in malice.
Our primary woe is reputation;
If now with child, I'd have thy palace
As her new station, her pleasure and home.
30   And since these new pains came through his savour
She should need a partner, a princely groom
To comfort her in full pregnant labour
And father the Prince within her new womb.

21

In short, my Liege, my vengeance is carried
If you consent to see them both married.
RUFUS. So be it then, let Phoebe be his bride
And we shall them wed ere the third high tide.
ISOBEL. Yet we could do better not to command
The Prince take Phoebe, for one swift demand
40   Would certain ensure the opposite course
Should we try to guide his sweet hand perforce.
So let us instead play cupid and see
If we cannot change the wasp to a bee?
GRENALDO. Yet how should she Valentino allure,
For she thinks the innocent and the pure?
She knows not how to entrap his quick heart;
Meet they again he might tear her apart!
ISOBEL. Your Queen shall then train her to be more wise
In manner and sense with cunning replies.

                                Exit Isobel and Grenaldo.

50   RUFUS. By Jove as my witness, I'll have an heir;
My son shall wed, be it fair or unfair!

                                    Exeunt.

II.2   *Enter Valentino.*
VALENTINO. Tell me, dear friends, for I think of ye so,
How is't I should live, truly I would know?
Should I worship my father and blindly
Concede to serve but him, to 'sue his lead
No matter of my wants, desires, needs
To exact my youth, to sow my own seeds?
And of this thing love of which poets speak,
What is its purpose, wherefore do they seek
To make but one victim of their jealous hearts
10   When there are three billion others to part?
Why then transfix, chain thy fear to one soul?
'Twill not God persuade, nor flatter, cajole
To grant thee more time, to live once again;
When the breath is out there is no Eden.
Religion? Ha! A synonym of Hell!
I wonder that God has so much to sell?
How rich must the church be before it's time
To purge itself and confess its own crime?
'Tis all a crutch, a device to breed fear
20   To keep us beneath true sinners, 'tis clear.
Wherefore trust to some cabbage leaf story

When all they lust is power and glory?
Create in our image master of all?
It cannot be true, for we are too small,
Yet too immodest to see the plain truth,
So we brain-wash ourselves and our poor youth
To believe in that which cannot be proved;
How very convenient, God would approve!
Nay, I choose to live loose of this madness,
30   That I am one is the only sadness.
Label me selfish, a cheat or a sod,
Freedom is my master, mistress and God!

Enter Barthes and Jaques.

JAQUES. Valentino, my Lord, we bring great news,
For long have we thought and shaken our muse
And perchance we have thee the perfect bride.
Go now, Barthes, and entreat her inside.

                                        Exit Barthes.

She is the finest woman of the land,
Of the highest bill and in great demand.
Her eyes, the essence of Heaven on earth
40   That upon all who view comes wondrous mirth.
Her lips impart the most delicate rush
Bestowing rapture, together they blush.
Her cheeks are liken to those of a babe,
The locks of her hair consent in cascades.
Her bosom is ample, more than a palm,
Her waist as thin as the script of a psalm.
She's perfection wrapped in female form;
The illicit flame, the eye o' the storm!
There is none better as many could tell,
50   May I hereby present Miss Jezebel.

Enter Jezabel and Barthes.

(*Aside to Valentino*) Now, she was a whore until this morning,
But for thee a whole new world is dawning.
VALENTINO. A whore, Jaques? Why, what means thee by this?
JAQUES. I beg thee have faith; forgiveness is bliss!
BARTHES. Come, good Jaques, let us leave them apart;
Strange meetings can oft awaken strange hearts.

                                Exit Barthes and Jaques.

VALENTINO. Thou art the fairest, 'tis my confession.
How is't you entered this sad profession?
JEZABEL. Forgive me, sir, but how wouldst thou like it?

VALENTINO. Pardon?

60 JEZABEL.   Those others who brought me hither,
Conveyed thy need of relations to know;
Promised me gold, that I may for thee be
A quiver to place thy amorous bow.
VALENTINO. You speak the tongue of a business guru,
Yet have I no change, do you take Euro?
JEZABEL. 'Tis said thou art now forced into marriage
Against thy will and without thy heart, yet
How would it be if within thy carriage
You held the sweet hand of love but in part?

70 VALENTINO. Forgive my seemingly innocent mind,
But thy meaning I cannot seem to find.
JEZABEL. Union for thee, 'tis said, would be hell;
Confined by law to a solitary bed,
Yet nightly thou might'st betroth Jezebel
If as thy wife she enrapture thy head.
VALENTINO. I am a Prince, I could ne'er match a whore.
JEZEBEL. Then marry not, but negotiate well
The terms and setting to sweeten thy store.
VALENTINO. Pray tell, what is't thou art craving to sell?

80 JEZEBEL. A life, my Lord, for I see thee too well.
In truth you await for perfection's bride,
A lady honest enough to be fair;
A virtuous maid you might stand beside,
Yet would she thee honour with trust and care?
Love may be a many splendorous thing
To poets and knights who live but in dreams
And have yet to taste the black pain it brings,
The lies, the jealously and darker themes.
Soft poets paint cupid as golden light;

90 'Tis a fool that writes of love without sight!
She is not blind of the judgements we take,
Love is defined by the reasons we make!
Think thee upon each new love thou hast felt,
Was't her heart or thine that caused thee to melt?
Methinks in daylight you'll find it was thine,
So why continue thyself to decline
The truth of owning a mere human heart?
We're born to love, then grow slowly apart.
'Tis natural for man and woman alike,

100 So let us be friends and do as we like.

24

As thy wife I'd love thee and be thy mate,
Honour, cherish and copulate, yet should
Thee chance desire another, thy friend
Would oblige her, not thee over smother.
'Tis natural for all men to spread their seed
And stands 'gainst nature to wish them recede
Since love is a feeling that lives within,
Not drawn from another thence to begin.
'Tis within our pure hearts the live long day
110 With only our minds to hold it at bay,
So tame thy brain and love thou shalt feel,
Without the need of her at thy heel.
       He kisses her.
VALENTINO. 'Tis wondrous true! I'll impart to the King
The nonpareil news of our near wedding.
JEZABEL. O! Rufus, the King?
VALENTINO.   Sometime my father.
       He kisses her again.
JEZEBEL. There is perhaps one thing I should mention.
VALENTINO. Later, my love, break not the suspension!
                          Exeunt.

II.3   *Enter Jaques and Barthes.*
JAQUES. O what where we thinking, playing cupid?
My master will kill me; I'm so stupid!
BARTHES. There goes the Prince now in hand with the whore.
       Jaques faints.
Jacques! What fainted? Jaques, don't ignore!
       Bathes Slaps Jacques
Enter Lady Maria.
       MARIA. Barthes, my late servant, where hast thou been
And why dost thou beat the Prince's servant?
Yet no matter, make thyself now unseen.
                      Exit Barthes.
Perchance this fell action is heaven sent?
Now to punish my love Valentino,
10 By desperate means; a sexual pinch.
Never again shall the Prince tell me no,
I'll lower myself 'pon his servant's inch!
       Maria slaps Jaques.
Awake Jaques and do as I bid thee:
Unbuckle thy wears, quickly then give me
Thy amorous shaft, thy great knightly sword!

25

Another slap.

Come hurry thee boy, I must be adored!

JAQUES. Forgive me, my Lady, art thou yet well?

I'm not Valentino, can you not tell?

Another slap.

MARIA. Be quiet you fool, I'll take what I please,

20   Now open thy drawers; be swift do not tease!

JAQUES. For the love of Mary, have you turned mad?

(Aside) Aristocracy today, it's really

Quite sad!

Another slap.

MARIA. To whom do you speak, thy master

Is here, do my bidding else die in fear!

JAQUES. *(Aside)* I live in fear of the upper classes,

So please you Lady, do you need glasses?

I am Valentino's servant Jaques!

Another slap.

MARIA. Speak not, thou lackey, my lust you'll appease!

JAQUES. My Lady relent, for love of mercy;

30   Nay, I'll not do it, lay off my percy!

They wrestle.

MARIA. Give me thy trumpet!

JAQUES.   Nay, pull not my bow!

MARIA. Make me thy strumpet!

Enter Marcello, armed.

JAQUES.   Madame, do not blow;

No words of lust more from thy tainted lips!

Coming forth.

MARCELLO. Desist and cease sir, I have thee a point.

MARIA. O thanks, kind sir, he was grabbing my bits!

JAQUES. What? How dare thee! She was after my joint!

Marcello slaps Jaques.

MARCELLO. Speak not thou butcher, I saw with mine eyes

Thy lusting and raping, do not add lies

To the list of crimes I now shall report

40   My father Grenaldo, of the King's court.

JAQUES. Look, I'm Prince Valentino's headman!

Marcello slaps Jaques.

MARCELLO.   Liar!

Fear not, sweet Lady, I'll do all I can

To see this felon is brought to justice.

MARIA. O how couldst I ever thank thee for this?

MARCELLO. 'Tis nought, my Lady, being a soldier.
MARIA. A warrior true, look at those shoulders!
So firm thou must be in mind and muscle,
(Undoing her dress) Such mighty hands – O, look at my bustle!
T'hath come undone by this animal's paws.
50   JAQUES. I tell thee straight she was inside my drawers!
        Marcello slaps Jaques repeatedly.
MARCELLO. No more slander or thy life is undone!
MARIA. *(Aside)* Such a masterful tone, strong as the sun!
I pray, good sir, wouldst thou help to redress
My wares and all that did cover my breast?
JAQUES. *(Aside)* What a slut!
        Marcello beats Jaques.
MARCELLO.   Hold thy tongue abhorrent mutt!
My Lady, I'll take this villain to court,
Then perchance we'll try adding one and nought.
MARIA. I'm sure thy sum doth arouse a figure
Of greater proportion, so much bigger!
JAQUES. *(Aside)* For God's sake!
        Marcello beats Jaques harder.
60   MARCELLO.   Come, I tire of his japes,
   Let us swift to the king, then to thy drapes!
                  Exeunt.

II.4   *Enter King, Queen, Don Grenaldo, Phoebe.*
   RUFUS. Bethink thee straight this court plan will succeed
In trapping the Prince and serving our need?
GRENALDO. Brother, in sooth, I am breeding just this:
'Tis risk, assured, but to cease is to miss.
ISOBEL. Now remember, Phoebe, as we thee taught,
Draw then detach and the Prince shall be caught.
PHEOBE. So please, your Highness, I'll act out my best,
To benet his heart and so pass this test.
ISOBEL. Very well, child, let what may be pass;
10   Keep strong thy will and remember our class.
PHEOBE. Aye, Madame.
GRENALDO.   Hasten, the Prince doth approach!
RUFUS. Come all and swiftly, so not to encroach.
GRENALDO. Behind the arras let us take our view,
To direct and re-guide this scene anew.
        The King, Queen and Don Grenaldo hide.
Enter Valentino.
   VALENTINO. Ah, sweet Phoebe, hast thou seen my father?

I bring great news, yet prithee, art thou well?
PHEOBE. Forgive me, my Lord, as I would rather
Not speak to thee lest my ankles soon swell.
VALENTINO. I offend thee?
PHEOBE.   Nay, my Lord, I defend
20   Myself for honour, duty and for health.
GRENALDO. O she is already so much better!
ISOBEL. Quiet, signor, do not her unfetter.
VALENTINO. I must be contrite if I have discalmed
Thy fair peace of mind or thy person harmed.
PHEOBE. Many thanks for these pains, my yet kind Lord.
VALENTINO. A maid in distress can ne'er be ignored.
PHEOBE. A maid, I was, yet I am now not so
And in sooth 'bout my duties I must go.
GRENALDO. O, mark this! Mark this, I say!
RUFUS.   Hush thee!
ISOBEL.   Peace!
30   VALENTINO. Yet, good cousin, I would see thee contented,
Be there ought to have love and thee augmented?
PHEOBE. Should I find the words, thou wouldst but bemock;
My catch hath been picked, pray do not deride!
VALENTINO. I could yet act as the key to thy lock;
Open thy mortise, in safety confide.
PHEOBE. There's but one thing that I would desire.
VALENTINO. Aye?
PHEOBE.   'Tis to see the Prince, thou, my sire,
Cradle that soul 'tis now said grows within,
Then bind our life as another begins.
GRENALDO. O what say ye? She is my daughter!
40   RUFUS and ISOBEL.   Hush!
VALENTINO. O Phoebe, poor Phoebe, would that I could,
Yet I know nought of the matters I should.
If circumstance is as thou doth protest
I offer pity, but could not contest
To be unto thee ought but a brother,
For in truth I've just vowed myself to another.
GRENALDO. What's this, what's this?
RUFUS.   Why, this is bliss!
ISOBEL.   'Tis bliss!
VALENTINO. As my second, indeed, I would thee wed,
For thou art the purest that I've misled.
50   Take comfort in this: if she lived no more,

I would thyself and thy babe much adore.
>*He kisses her.*

The rest come forward.

GRENALDO. How now, *indignus*! Hands off my daughter!
ISOBEL. Phoebe, my dear, go take of some water.
>*Exit Phoebe.*

RUFUS. Grenaldo! Brother, becalm thee at once!
GRENALDO. I should rip out thine eyes thou perfumed ponce!
VALENTINO. Tame this old fool 'fore I learn him some grace.
GRENALDO. Come hither, thou dog, say that to my face!
RUFUS. Enough Grenaldo, consider thy state,
Thy dutiful mind and our swift rebate
60 Should thee yet persist in causing affray;
Satisfaction shall pass, do not dismay.
Thy daughter may not now live to be Queen,
Yet well ye shall fare, when all has been seen.
GRENALDO. I am, as ever, thy servant, my Lord.
RUFUS. Then rest thee calm, set thy mind in accord.
Now, Valentino, my sweet Prince, my son
Speak more on this girl; you have found the one?
VALENTINO. 'Tis true, father, I deem she's ideal
To raise the standards, to meet thy seal.
RUFUS. What be her position?
70 ISOBEL. Aye, has she wealth?
VALENTINO. Her service is wide, her fortune is stealth
RUFUS. Yet what's her title, might one enquire?
ISOBEL. Is it that nice girl, Lady Maria?
VALENTINO. Nay, dearest mother, she'd drive me to hell,
Instead I present the fair Jezebel.

Enter Jezebel.

JEZEBEL. Your majesties.
RUFUS. But, yet, nay! This cannot be!
ISOBEL. O husband, what now? What is it with thee?
VALENTINO. Aye, good father, be there something amiss?
RUFUS. 'Tis just, why she – O you can't marry this!
80 ISOBEL. Forgive me, Rufus, but hasten to tell
If there be cause to not choose Jezebel.
She seems like a sweet girl; her looks are fair,
What better choice for creating an heir?
RUFUS. *(Aside).* The devil take me, for I cannot say,
'Twould but serve in giving myself away.
(To Isobel) Why, nothing, dear wife, she's the perfect match.

29

          A good choice my son, a wondrous catch!

          VALENTINO. *(Aside).* Methinks I just caught my father sleeping.

          RUFUS. Valentino, from now, no more creeping!

               Valentino and Rufus laugh.

90   ISOBEL. Speak then, my dear child, tell us thy mind,

          Wilt thou consent to so marry in kind?

          JEZEBEL. The honour is mine to have such fortune,

          I assure my service shall ne'er cause ye

          Importune.

          ISOBEL.   An honest and quaint reply.

          What say you husband, can we her deny?

          RUFUS. *(Aside).* Bitterest fate, this cannot be real;

          A whore for a daughter, a half-eaten

          Meal!

          ISOBEL. Husband? King! Art thou yet in peace?

          Que dis tu à Jezebel et ton fils?

100   RUFUS. What? Ah yes, of our son and this Lady?

          (Aside) Must I do something to save me this hell.

          (To Isobel) I'm not sure she's suited to handle a

          Baby. Listen, my Prince, and hear me well:

          I'faith, she maybe too old or barren.

          What of that Sophie, Sarah or Sharron?

          VALENTINO. I care nought for those girls, this is my bride.

          ISOBEL. She seems well able; why, look at those thighs!

          RUFUS. Yet what of her stock and category,

          We know nothing of her but that we see?

110   VALENTINO. I assure thee father, she knows her place,

          Shall cost us no dribbling, nor no disgrace.

          She is most duteous, I'm sure you've seen,

          All things to a man and ever so keen.

          RUFUS. I had as lief you marry Grenaldo!

          ISOBEL. What breaches thy mind is what I would know?

          E'er long hast thou wished our son to be wed,

          To curb his craving and temper his needs.

          To sow himself unto one in his bed,

          So serving to that upon which thou feeds,

120   Yet when our son hath chosen a vessel

          Cording to the prescript that thou beheld,

          Some else in thy mind doth swift un-nestle!

          What more can he do to thy metal meld?

          Wherefore dost thou now then question his choice?

          Should you have fair grounds, pray give them thy voice.

Enter Marcello, Maria and Jaques.

    MARCELLO. Father Grenaldo, your majesties all,
    I bring thee a villain and a tale
    To appaul the hearts and minds of those who
    Would hear it, for the infirm of nature
130   It may not be fit. For here is a man
    Of such base-like depravity, of great
    Unspeakable sin and vice, the devil
    Himself would float above his gravity
    Calling him master, he doth so crime entice!
    'Twas but a few moments hence I captured
    This slave, his hands 'pon and in this lady
    Like in madness he did rave, and even
    As I him took, innocence he protested,
    Claiming it was he by her who'd been so
140   Savagely molested! He then laid claim
    To be the Prince's chief head servant, yet
    Another lie of course, so I hard prat
    'Till he repent. Following soon after
    Came a torrent of abuse, he must be
    Subject to a fool, from what I can deduce,
    For he would not a moment cease in so
    Attacking this poor Lady, naturally
    I him beat and fleece till he whimpered like
    A baby. Finally, I would but add
150   One addition to his file, he cut
    My knuckles twice when I him smashed within
    His smile! Knowing the gaols be full,
    My Lords, I brought him straight to court, so may
    This fiend be brought to bear and his sad life
    Reduced to nought.
    JAQUES.   Master, I did nothing!
        Marcello slaps Jaques.
    MARCELLO. Speak not fool, in the presence of the King!
    VALENTINO. Enough, Marcello, lest from thy neck I
    Have thee swing. Come hither, Jaques, let the
    Servant seek his master, we'll escort thee
160   To our lodge and render thee with plaster.
                Exit Valentino, Jezebel and Jaques.
    MARCELLO. Forgive me, yet, I do not understand.
    I swear, upon my honour, I did he
    From her withstand.

ISOBEL.   In sooth, gentle nephew,
We do much thank thee for thy kind duty
And here rend thee rewards, for thy hard pains
A generous booty. Yet know thee this,
And I pray all present savour, Jaques,
For such was thy prisoner's name, slaves for
Nothing but our favour. As too did his
170   Good father and another one before;
A more tried and trusted line of servants
There never was before. Through this hard bond
And kinship we did place him with the Prince
To guard our only saviour and have ne'er
Regretted since. So by virtue of these
Sure facets, we can but learn one lesson:
Somewhere along the hazy path ye gained
The wrong impression. Perhaps 'twas but he
Did saunter in his sleep or chance zealous
180   Maria him misconstered somewhat deep?
Whate'er may have passed 'tis now but vanished
Into air, so I pray all about their
Business and of this matter let us care.
MARCELLO. But, your Majesty -
GRENALDO.   Peace! Less of nothing!
Forgive my son's o'erhasty line, let me
Instead here take the time to re-incline
His heart and manner towards the stuffing.
RUFUS. Carry on, brother Grenaldo.
GRENALDO.   My Lord.
               Exit Rufus, Isobel, Guards and Attendants.
MARCELLO. O my father, I beg thee have a care,
190   This is justice blind; it simply isn't fair!
GRENALDO. Have patience, my son, all shall be made right.
Lady Maria, I see the Prince hath
Lost thy sight.
MARIA.   'Tis most true, my noble Lord,
I have been hard punished for my labours.
Enter Phoebe, unseen.
GRENALDO. How wouldst thou like a chance to thus return
His Lordship's favours?
MARIA.   I pray thee, speak on.
GRENALDO. Listen to me close, thence stir not any
Region of the air to be hence witness

To our intrigue. So grant me thy depose,
200   For should this stratagem be paired the King
Would hang all parts in league.
MARIA.   I swear.
MARCELLO.   So I.
GRENALDO. 'Afore ye did arrive I did o'erhear
The Prince in speaking, he spake upon his
Bride and of the love that he was seeking,
Yet in truth he's found a girl that any
Could adore, her name be Jezebel, she's
A vixen and a whore! I sense the stench o'
Convenience doth circle 'bout their wedding,
Know I she was for sale since I oft
210   Hired for the King. But should this lowly
Jade make her swift exit from our story,
As Valentino said himself, he would
Take Phoebe as his glory; therefore, as
Sister to the Queen thou couldst have all that
Thou desired, a palace or greater
Title should'st thee be that way inspired.
All that needs be done is to rid Florence
Of a flea, in that I ask thy aidence
So tend and water unto me. 'Tis sure
220   The Prince is now at home with his servant
And his whore, so let ye pay a visit
And to our headache find a cure. Take thy
Headman Barthes to occupy his equal,
Thus leaving you to challenge Valentino
To a sequel. Whilst in this fiery scene
Marcello here will enter, find the room
Of Jezebel and thence to hell will he
Sure send her.
MARCELLO. Father, of what dost thou speak?
I could never kill a Lady.
GRENALDO.   Listen
230   To me boy, thy sister carries in her
Womb the Prince's bastard baby! 'Twas achieved
When he didst her rape and violate, so
Speak not to me of morals! Intend I
To swift usurp this crown; this monarchy
I'll ground, like a ship upon chaste corals.
MARCELLO. I am my father's most steadfast servant.

GRENALDO. Maria, what thinks ye 'pon our gambit?
MARIA.   Methinks the time hath come to out these pains
Into remit.
GRENALDO. Come then, let us now act
240   And so from hence all profit from this pact.

Exeunt all but phoebe.

PHOEBE. O hateful future, now is Phoebe lost,
For though my father tread the flames 'twill be
My love that counts the cost. Gravest censure!
To face the choice 'tween kith and closest kin,
Twix bitterest virtue and sweetest sin!
O swift decision, let instinct take my guide;
I shall present all case and in judgement
He'll preside. On my father's part, he means
Me well, yet his prospect ranks with evil;
250   To plot the loss of any life betrays
Corruption of thy will. As for my Prince,
Though his heart to me be not attracted,
I do love him still, as I have so long,
And from his world would ne'er be extracted.
In sooth, I'd not beteem the voice of God
Within his pure soul to speak too deeply,
For I do him with hunger grow, though my
Tongue 'splay this un-neatly. O cunning fate!
That chance would have me pass this hall as if
260   To test my courage. Wherefore could I here
Derogate 'gainst that my sense encourage?
So now, strong Phoebe, take thy spirit to
This matter, of thy father, brother and
The Prince, thou belongeth to the latter.
Go then, and bewarn him of thy father's
Malcontent, to thyself be always true
Or end this life in deep repent. My love!

Exeunt.

III.1   *Enter Jaques in bandages.*
JAQUES. Women! O how I have paid for my sin!
Methinks perchance Valentino is right,
Entrust a woman and day becomes night!
Look me, in small bits and pieces I am,
'Twas grave sacrifice that rib of Adam!
'Tis lucky my master trust not their race,
So gave not a second thought to her case,

34

Yet 'tis fearful to sense the weight they hold;
One salted speech and thy future is sold.
10   I will not lie, this session hath changed me,
From hence the Prince's second shall I be.
What needs a man to stay with a Lady?
She has but one job: conceive thy baby!
The rest is a waste of both mind's muscle;
A long breed apart are women and men.
Why spend a life in pitiful tussle?
You would not encage a dog and a hen!
Wherefore then race to habit together?
Sunshine with rain is yet still foul weather!
20   Both sexes have separate parts to enact,
Enchaining each other inhibits, distracts,
Breaks the mind from its greater achievements
'Till the old cuckold cries, dies and repents.
But not now me, I shall ne'er be broken,
I'll live without if these be their token.
Yet, in sooth, I thank Lady Maria,
Now I'll live to enthuse and inspire
All people to live with love in their heart,
Yet distant from that which itself could part.

Enter Phoebe running.

30   PHOEBE. O Lord! Dear Jaques, where be thy master?
Yet, you poor thing, all covered in plaster!
Pray tell, what became of thy limbs and legs
To resemble such matter as cotton
And eggs?
JAQUES. 'Twas gentle Lady Maria
Enticing me to crown her Empire.
PHOEBE. Right. Yet tell me straight, where's Valentino,
For of certain things I hear he must know?
JAQUES. He ventured to town with his bride to be.
Becalm thee poor girl, what is't plaguing thee?
40   PHOEBE. O, dear Jaques, I fear I cannot say
Lest my heart here break with painful dismay.
I must but speak these hard words to the Prince,
As they stick in my throat like uncooked mince.
JAQUES. Then rest a while, my poor little sweet,
For thee I'll retrieve the Prince in a beat.
PHOEBE. Much thanks, kind Jaques, I shall repose;
In truth, I'm so vexed, I need a quick doze!

Act III, scene 1

       JAQUES. Sweet dreams then, I'll return by eleven
       Then ye shall rise and wake to thy heaven.
          Phoebe sleeps.   *Exit Jaques.*
Enter Marcello, with a dagger.
50   MARCELLO. How now, what's this, all alone and apart?
       Why I need not the others to temper
       This heart. Who would bethink it? The Prince's
       Whore sleeps as soft as an angel hails tears
       When she weeps. And see how her hair glissades
       To one side; such innocent looks could well
       Pass for a bride. The pegs of a Princess,
       A short little span. Ye would not believe
       She's a cheap courtesan! So refrain thee
       Marcello, consider thy work, think not
60   Of the deed but the family perk, for
       With one swift blow shall I reset our fate.
       Now stick to thy course, do not hesitate,
       Nor act thee barren of strength my good hand,
       Be at my setting, my will and command.
       Yet how wouldst I be if one murdered my
       Sister? O think not fool! Thy mind 'twill blister
       The skin of thy dagger's sure intent, being
       Thus far we cannot relent! Come then, boy,
       And regain thy sense of duty! 'Tis but
70   A piece of meat; a means to wealth and beauty!
       So this I do for my gentle Phoebe,
       Who would die o fright if she could see me.
       Go whore, in peace, and pray do not me blame;
       I'll cure thy soul and release thee from shame.
          Marcello stabs Phoebe.
       There, there, my sweet, I'll at least make it swift;
       Try not to resist, to God ye must drift!
       Yet one cut more in thy still beating heart.
       Nay, do not fight, from this world ye must part!
          Marcello stabs Phoebe again.
       There now, 'tis done, so my sister's beset
80   To receive her Lord; her crown to beget.
       Yet 'tis best I check this corpse hath no breath,
       Ye can ne'er be too careful when dealing
       In death!
          Marcello drops the dagger.
       O gravest sin! What is't I have done?

Nay, 'tis a dream! Nay! Sister, fordone?
Yet speak, O sister! Phoebe, wherefore?
How can this be? Wherefore? Yet, wherefore?
I have here murdered my sister, my blood!
This cannot be real, I must be asleep;
90   I'm but in a vision too powerfully deep
And the devil has taken my heart for a drum!
Anon, someone comes, whilst I come undone!

                   Exit Marcello.

Enter Jaques.

     JAQUES. Fret thee not Phoebe, for the Prince arrives
Soon ye may tell what's behind those sad eyes.
Phoebe? O Poor girl! What, will ye not stir?
A deeply grave slumber, I must concur.
Yet wake thee child, prepare for the Prince.
What ho? Nay, murdered? Taken just since?
O sweet Phoebe! Here the bloody dagger,
100   All covered in sweat of the villain that
Drag her! O my child, would that I could
Fix thee and thy poor babe that shall sleep
With thee featly.

Enter Jezebel. She screams.

Enter Valentino, drawn.

     VALENTINO. What ho, Jezebel? Jaques, I profess!
O, what is't thou hast done? Come now, confess!
     JAQUES. Nay! Why nay, my master, 'tis not my hand.
     VALENTINO. Yet speaketh no more, I late understand;
Maria was earnest, thou hast turned mad!
Nay, lie no more devil, be thee most glad
110   I sell not thy life, *caveat emptor!*
Now grace thy grave weapon unto the floor.
     JAQUES. Master!
     VALENTINO.   I say release thy bloodiest blade!
        Jaques drops the dagger.
     JAQUES. My Lord, I implore -
     VALENTINO.   No words more shall 'suade
Nor taint our ear, thou shalt be hanged for this
Jaques, that much is clear. Hold thee. Guards! Guards!
Enter Guards.

     Arrest this servant for murder most foul.
     JEZEBEL. I fear him, my Lord, see how he doth scowl!
     JAQUES. My Lord, I swear, this crime I did not do.

VALENTINO. Of course, like Maria, she attacked you!
120 JAQUES. Nay, nay, my Prince, why I left her dozing.
VALENTINO. At rest indeed, now ever reposing.
Take this beast well out of our sight!
JAQUES.   My Lord!
Nay! Nay, my Lord!

Exit Jacques under guard.

VALENTINO.   Sweet harmony's discord!
Mine uncle will sure seek retaliation,
For the acts of one kept within our station.
So must I grant us the gift of time. Guards!
With utmost safety, by passage sublime
Bare secret this body unto our halls,
Ere a father's revenge like darkness falls.

Exit Guards and Jezebel.

130 I must then grow and act with good concord;
For sake of the whole this part shall accord.

Exeunt.

III.2 *Enter Rufus.*

RUFUS. Contriving fortune! Didst I thee implore
To thus crag the footholds of my future?
That mine only heir should betroth a whore;
'Tis great misconduct he doth now venture!
Wherefore must I 'dure this bitter-sweet state
When I have governed both fairly and kind?

Enter Isobel, unseen by Rufus.

Be this the salary, the swift rebate
For actions impure that chance doth remind?
Alas, 'tis true, I have known Jezebel;
10 O foulest crime, to con thy new daughter!
How canst Valentino thrive in this hell?
Should the Queen glean 'twould safe be my slaughter.
I have sith witnessed the strength of her scorn,
In sooth, this country my passing would mourn!
Yet, my grandson, a whoreson? This cannot .
He must think of our future, our lineage
And me! The Prince shall not marry the jade
Jezebel, an offence of this nature
Would heaven compel to reject our name
20 At Peter's entry, leaving royal blood
To waste sedimentary. Yet, peace, who stirs?

Exit Isobel.

Grenaldo, do ye pace? My Queen, my love,
Be thee in this place? 'Twas merely the wind;
The mind betrays when the body has sinned.
Have I my future sold with ancient lies
And pricked too much the short sides of pity,
To be worthy of the smallest reprise?
I beg thee Lord, an heir for this city.

Noises off.

Yet who is't disquiets our peaceful palace?

Enter Valentino, Jezebel, and Guards bearing the body of Phoebe.

30   VALENTINO. Father, grave tidings follow hard upon.

          Valentino embraces his father.

RUFUS. Cease not to impart my new loving son.
VALENTINO. Methinks perchance good Marcello spoke sooth
When imparting the whisper, now held sans
Reproof, of our servant Jaques' crime;
O gravest play! 'Twas a sad paradigm,
For his last act hath put beyond reproach
Sure need for en-keeping; his freedom must
We encroach since now he raves in madness
Too unsubtle, as Phoebe discovered

40   When he did her murder by this cuttle.
Such was his hatred opposing their race
He cut out her heart, inscribed in its place
The signature of the devil himself;
Perchance, being bought, he drudge for the Guelph?
That papal sect, that hated, strive counter,
Would laugh should we fall through this encounter.
A device of such black cunning as this!
Don Grenaldo's daughter, his sweetness, his bliss
Savagely slaughtered within our sanctum;

50   *Bene nox* thence to those of our kingdom!
I warn thee, father, the Don's vengeance shall
Stay sharp; had we the villain caught only
To free thence her to jarp. Must we rest all
Other matters to bed, 'till we vouchsafe
Ourselves a future; save our common head.
RUFUS. 'Tis agreed and unequivocally so.
VALENTINO. Then let us brief hold this grave news of late,
For I would fain thy half-brother not know
'Till of a device we confabulate.

60   Let Jezebel guard her within thy cell,
         'Till intelligence doth danger dispell.
         JEZEBEL. Had I rather venture with thee, my Lord.
         VALENTINO. For these smallest pains, a lifetime's reward.
             He kisses her putting a ring on her finger.
         Guards! Install this corpse in chamber of the King,
         That none should see lest they bear the royal ring.
         GUARD. Aye, my Lord.
             The guards bear out the body of Phoebe. Exit Jezebel.
         VALENTINO. Come father, let us now set to toil,
         A rancorous covert plot to foil.
                                  Exit Valentino.
         RUFUS. *(Aside)* Chance all is not lost within these trials;
70   The son now greets the father with smiles!
                                  Exeunt.

III.3   *Enter Grenaldo, Maria and Barthes.*
         GRENALDO. Speak again, Lady, of that ye bespoke.
         MARIA. In sooth, my Lord, Marcello was absent
         In spirit and body; his will did choke.
         For too long an hour we him forewent
         At the Prince's gate, thy spirit to serve,
         Yet nothing would stir, ergo nought should pass,
         Since without thy son we could not subserve
         To cleanse the blood that we might then surpass.
         GRENALDO. O seedless fruit! Shall none yield a feast?
10   Ye have not then, I pray, seen our son since?
         BARTHES. Of all thy minion we saw him the least.
         Yet what must pass 'twix this girl and the Prince?
         GRENALDO. Leave unto me, I shall guide their passing.
         Peace! Go, depart! Swift steps come amassing.
                         Exit Maria and Barthes.
Enter the Queen.
         ISOBEL. Grenaldo.
         GRENALDO.   Thy servant.
         ISOBEL.   Nay, I am thine.
             They kiss.
         GRENALDO. How now, furtive love, what news weighs thy head?
         ISOBEL. I am betrayed, certain mocked by design,
         Even by those lips 'pon which I once fed.
         GRENALDO. The King deceives thee?
         ISOBEL.   Aye, as much as we
20   That did so many moons violate trust,

For our daughter to be, my son's chosen bride,
Was once the King's whore; his vision of lust!
GRENALDO. Nay, Isobel, why it cannot be so!
ISOBEL. I heard him this in confession confide.
The bitter-sweet souvenirs of his crime
Now torment his mind, his conscience divide
And hath not the stomach to aid in chyme.
GRENALDO. What wouldst thou, my love?
ISOBEL.   Revenge, plain and true.
GRENALDO. 'Pon thy husband the king?
ISOBEL.   Nay, we are through.

30   By my heart, I know our insults equal;
So cull the whore to avoid a sequel!
Unbind this foul knotting, put her in hell;
As I am thy love, so slay Jezebel!
Thence this fair Queen shall become only thine,
Never again thy sweet bed to decline,
Since with this death so dies all condition.
GRENALDO. Should I thee aid 'twould but welcome suspicion;
Thus, I'll but provide the means to thy will,
Should thee so wish thou may then do her ill.

40   Taketh this vile, the contents therein
If mixed with water doth fuse a toxin
So potent and fleet 'fore draining the glass
The drinker thereafter shall speed and pass.
ISOBEL. Much thanks, sweet lover, I shall make good use.
GRENALDO. Beware, my Queen, its power is shocking,
Deserving respect in place of abuse.
Once entered the blood there is no blocking;
No earthly device could save the taker
From losing their soul unto their maker.

50   ISOBEL. 'Tis unconscious knowledge that some must die;
A world of peace is a world full of lies.
GRENALDO. Once 'tis done, I pray the royal seal
Might see Phoebe at the Prince's heel?
ISOBEL. Fear not, faithful Don, we know our station
And shall set her forth in approbation.
    They kiss.   *Exit Isobel.*
GRENALDO. Kind fate, it seems, doth place her hand 'pon mine,
Augmenting my power through will Divine.
So speed her thither to set in motion
My greatest conquest by smallest potion.
                              Exit Grenaldo.

III.4   *Enter Jezebel with Guards bearing the body. Exit Guards.*
         JEZEBEL. Pitiable Phoebe, to be reduced
         By the plague of man and his desire;
         Still young and tender and yet so abused,
         Such is the ending our times inspire.
         Innocent fledgling, Jacques' victim,
         What grave passion could have taken him thus
         To gut and defile such a seraphim?
         Proud fury, no doubt, and the creature lust
         Did rise 'pon his back and swiftly arouse,
10   Igniting his blood-hunt, dulling his brains.
         'Tis the fall of man that his senses drowse;
         When heeding envy mere instinct remains.
         What a wonderful piece of work is man,
         How noble to chase the call of Heaven!
         Yet how rank and base to then bend God's plan
         To serve their will through the deadly seven.
         With a grin they sin, misquoting scriptures,
         False piety then the banner they fly;
         Nay, *God be with us*, they spread their dogma,
20   A saddening show; the religious lie.
         God is for love and ne'er for another,
         To be-claim his will on earth is untrue;
         When in hateful fear men murder their brother
         The emotional landscape of life is due.
         So sleep, fair Phoebe, angels shall thee guide
         To Zion's sweet state, e'er to rest inside.
                   She kisses her.

Enter Isobel.

         ISOBEL. What, already in my husband's chamber,
         Thou courtly vixen, with whom do you play?
         'Pon what poor mortal now do you partner
30   In lascivious impure lust, I pray?
         JEZEBEL. Nay, good Madame -
         ISOBEL.   Take not a pious tone!
         I hold thy crimes for which you'll ne'er atone.
         As I did chance to hear my King confess
         To that which his nature would hard repress.
         Aye, guilt is betrayed within thy feature,
         I swear, I ne'er thought to see a whore blush!
         O insolent, perfidious creature,
         With but these bare hands thy life I should crush!

(Aside) Now to entrap the too trusting strumpet;
40   I shall her play like a one note trumpet!
(To Jezebel) I should have thee tried for treason most high,
A charge thou knowst one can never deny,
Or broken upon my soldier's kind sword.
O how couldst thou covert, coerce my Lord?
Nay, utter no words, for my soul is weak,
Too kind and forgiving; it will not seek
To harm or injure any of God's flock.
O break my poor heart, 'tis such a base knock!
JEZEBEL. *(Kneeling)* Forgive me, my Lady, the buzz is true;
50   I wish there were somewhat that I may do
To perfect the past, or myself at least,
But time is the tamer of all poor beast
And has not yet served to grant me the chance
To alter the tune or amend this dance.
ISOBEL. Pray, who is this figure that will not budge
No matter the force or size of our grudge?
       Inspecting the body.
O! Nay! What treachery is upon this house?
O Phoebe, wherefore? All sense is displaced
As blackest fear stirs deep within my soul.
60   The future's misplaced; this weight is too much,
No mortal should suffer or venture such!
Darkness greater than hell itself could bear;
O give me some light, dear God give me air!
JEZEBEL. Seek peace, my Queen, for the Prince's prefer
The Don rest estranged from what has occurred.
ISOBEL. Speak thee no more thou unholy devil!
As this was thy doing, thou wilt be done.
       She takes out the poison.
(Aside) The storm must cease, the sea must be level;
All paths lead to her, she must be undone.
70   JEZEBEL. My Queen? My Lady? To whom dost thou speak?
ISOBEL. To the air, my child, give me thy beak.
JEZEBEL. Pardon, your majesty?
ISOBEL.   Thy lips, dear girl,
For I would part them in search of a pearl.
JEZEBEL. I do not understand, my Royal Queen?
ISOBEL. Come hither to me, pray don't make a scene!
JEZEBEL. What purpose, to see?
ISOBEL.   Do you question me?

JEZEBEL. 'Tis but thy function I cannot fathom.
ISOBEL. How dare ye disobey me, young Madame!
I do but wish to examine thy head
80 For marks of disease, so hop on the bed!
JEZEBEL. Forgive me my pause within this strange case,
Yet I would know where you'd locate my face?
ISOBEL. Why daughter, above thy shoulders, of course,
Now kneel before me, lest I use force!
JEZEBEL. *(Kneeling)* I shall then be as you yourself command.
ISOBEL. Breech wide thy dear mouth, now drink and be damned!
     Isobel forces the poison on Jezebel
Vilest nothing, get thee whence thou came!
Leave our kingdom. To hell! To hell for shame!
JEZEBEL. *(Dying)* O! Wherefore? What is't? Wherefore? O God!
90 ISOBEL. What's that my dear, has the reaper thy lung?
Thy short time hath passed, thy sweet song is sung!
Pray tell the devil to unattend me,
For with this kind act Heaven I shall see.
JEZEBEL. O!
ISOBEL.   What? Still here? Does it hurt? Does it smart?
Sense ye the poison corroding thy heart?
JEZEBEL. Please!
ISOBEL.   O short daughter, there's nought to be done,
But I'm so glad we talked; wasn't this fun?
Nearly there, I see, so take some advice,
In the next life to come try and be nice!
100 So farewell, adieu, I pray thee no peace;
May hell's everlasting torments ne'er cease!
     Jezebel dies.
God's will is done; our vengeance is carried.
Now to the quest of who shall be married
To mine only son, in whom do we trust?
What vessel to use continuing us?
Perchance I verse with Lady Maria,
For of rank and birth she is the higher?
But first to clear myself of this danger.
     Positioning Jezebel.
Rest ye there, like a babe in the manger!
110 The poison chalice firm within thy grasp,
A scream from me as I begin to gasp!
O! O! Guards, help me hither! O murder!
Enter Guards.

O! Murder! Murder! O!
  She faints.
GUARD.   Look to the Queen!
Enter Grenaldo.
  GRENALDO. Ho! Prithee, what stirs?
  GUARD.   Base treason, unseen.
  GRENALDO. Seek it out! Seek it out! How goes our Queen?
  GUARD. Fainted, yet well.
  GRENALDO.   'Scort her to my cover.
  GUARD. Aye, sir.
       Exit Guards supporting the Queen.
  GRENALDO. You sirs, bare out these other –
  Yet, who is't that hath passed?
  GUARD.   'Tis Jezebel,
  My Lord.
  GRENALDO. And t'other? I command thee speak!
  GUARD. My Lord, 'tis thy daughter, Phoebe.
120 GRENALDO.   Thou liest!
    Examining the body
  O mercy, sweet mercy! Whose hand was this?
  GUARD. Although no witness, as I understand,
  Thy daughter was slain by Jaques' hand.
  GRENALDO. Give me the chamber. Devils leave us now!
       Exit Guards bearing Jezebel.
  Peace be with thee, O my angel, good heart!
  So dies all pity, compassion and love,
  'Tis buried with thee, never to return;
  Vengeance shall now flood that void till I drown.
  O heaven and earth, how couldst ye permit?
130 I curse thee! No instrument of evil
  Shall hence remain unsheathed, as in the cold
  Black sleep of mourning beats our dark revenge.
  No hollow vault o'er deep, no sea too wide,
  No armour, nor field, no cross bearing
  Shall stay me my indissoluble course!
  Come God and assuage this I here declare:
  My enemies sworn, the Prince and the King,
  I curse hence to die and lie festering!
  Sound blackened drums upon my fearless heart,
140 Give turn to emptiness and death! O God
  Thou devil! Smite thee and thy septic host!
  There's no more music left but war, so play

On 'til we bleed. Rise proud fury, take up
In arms; give passing unto thy daughter sweet,
For no man, nor God, shall arrest this course
'Till bloodiest ending the Prince's meet.

Exit Grenaldo bearing Phoebe.

III.5   *Enter Maria and Barthes.*

BARTHES. Forgive me, my lady, I must recur,
To what sad affair did the Don refer
When he spoke 'pon, sorry to be asking,
Guiding the Prince and Jezebel's passing?
MARIA. Why, there be no cause to vex thy soft brain,
'Twas of their swift marriage; to ease the strain
The kind Don bethought it prudent to let
An extra porch, case the climate turns wet.
BARTHES. Yet, my Lady, 'tis midsummer's glory;

10   I chance to find this a likely story!
MARIA. Art thou now so bold to question my word?
BARTHES. 'Tis not of thee, but the Don have I heard
Rumours and tales t'would turn thy blood cold.
There be so many young 'twill ne'er grow old
By grace of the Don's so called charity;
I tell thee, he scares the pants off of me!
MARIA. Then perchance 'tis best ye speak not so loud,
Lest the Don hath spies placed within the crowd.
BARTHES. Of a truth, thou art right! 'Tis certainty,

20   For he sees far more than others can see.

Enter Guard.

GUARD. My Lady.
BARTHES. *(He draws)* Ah-ha! A mole in our midst!
I'll cut out thy heart! *(To Maria)* I told thee we didst.
MARIA. Pray, lower thy sword, 'tis but a report.
So tell me, good sir, what news from the court?
GUARD. Don Grenaldo would have thee for supper.
BARTHES. He'd eat us? For shame! Our lives to scupper!
O carnivorous crime! To end like this,
Served as a giblet of meat on his dish!
MARIA. Forgive my servant, his passion is fierce;

30   'Magination doth his reason transpierce!
Lead on, good sir, we follow with pleasure,
And haste to grace Don Grenaldo's leisure.

Exit Guard and Maria.

BARTHES. My Lady, do not! Lady Maria!

He'll spit roast thee alive on his fire!
Good heavens above, now what's to be done?
The Don will devour my Lady in one!
And I do suspect he intends foul play
'Pon the Prince and his intended this day.
I must, for honour, protect his highness
40   No matter the choice or cause of his bliss,
For without an heir to the throne in place
The Don might just somehow himself emplace.
Perhaps by a coup or Isobel's hand?
Aye, there's a line that has never been scanned!
I'fecks! If Grenaldo has woo'ed the Queen,
Then murders the King and the Prince unseen,
He would by default become the new King
And heaven only knows what that would bring!
A dark Lord like he chases one hour,
50   To hold, absolutely, absolute power.
And within that moment all hope is lost
As the innocent nations share the cost.
Murder is murder, in God's name or no,
I cannot allow this warmonger's show
To unchecked play his ill-verse 'pon our stage,
No matter the price or loss by his rage.
So by these words, I hereby pledge my life
To counter the Don and outwit his knife.

                                    Exit.

IV.1   *Enter The Prince, King and Officer.*
      VALENTINO. Father I tell thee again, 'tis assured,
Isobel by the Don is now allured.
Whose heart has grown subdued by such hunger
To see thee usurped, the foul whoremonger,
He will not rest till the kingdom is his,
Including thy wife and all her riches!
This officer here did observe the scene
Within thy chamber where Jezebel lay
Poisoned to death with no more than thy Queen
10   Beside her warm corpse, 'twas murder I say!
The motive is clear, as we two both know:
To destroy a once used sheath for thy bow!
I assume Grenaldo did pay the girl?
Such information could easy unfurl
About the ears of my vengeful mother,

47

Whom, if betrayed, would murder her brother
Rather than swallow or digest the shame;
Mine uncle hath cunningly played this game!
Now should misfortune come visiting us
20   He sure would be crowned without so much fuss,
For his weight is such within this city
That none should mourn or make show their pity
'Till he hath hastily thy wife re-wed
Thence to copulate on thy –
RUFUS.   Enough said!
Peace, I implore, my son for goodness sake,
Strive not to continue my heart to break!
VALENTINO. I do but seek to awake thy senses
To these foul and most cunning offences!
RUFUS. 'Tis awoken then, so pray give me pause
30   To contemplate and these crimes diapause.
VALENTINO. I urge thee father, we must act in haste
'Afore its too late and we are replaced!
RUFUS. Thou swear'st the Queen made way to his bedstead?
OFFICER. I swear, my Leige, by myself she was led.
Though not so much led, a more in leading;
Like worms to that upon which they're feeding
She knew the path like the back of her hand
And seemed at times pleased, as if she had planned
A hateful conquest upon some poor host,
40   Then spat on their grave and laughed at their ghost.
I could not say I was reading her mind,
Yet her 'haviour was a might odd I find.
'Pon installation within the Don's room
She preened herself, like a bride for her groom:
A swift measure here, a check in the glass
Am I at my best? How big is my –
VALENTINO.   Pass
These details, they are not for royal ears!
Stick to the plot that may confirm our fears.
OFFICER. Very well, my Prince, pardon my fervour,
50   I shall now, of this case, speak on further.
She ushered us then to leave her alone,
So about the door I thus placed myself.
When the Don went in, O how did she groan!
A constant hour she spoke to himself:
O God! O Lord! O you're such a baddie!

The reply came swift: *Now who's your daddy?*
Screaming the size I've ne'er heard before,
Save to remind me of a certain –
VALENTINO.   More
Function, less form is needed in thy wit;
60   Of the plans thou o'erheard, get to that bit!
OFFICER. Of course, my good Lord, these words I must primp,
I'll not even mention the Queen's late limp!
Instead we'll vault to the matter in hand:
The Don intends to take rule in this land,
This I have safe by Grenaldo's own lips;
He stood, much like this, his hands on his hips
And proclaimed forthwith his intentions to all:
To steal the crown and thy Queen to maul!
Of course, I do not quote him verbatim,
70   Yet such was the meat of his synonym.
This he spoke to all officers present,
I scarce believed their reaction was pleasant,
Though pleased they were, as if God were speaking;
Three cheers they raised and spoke of blood-seeking!
It seems the dark Lord hath muddied their mind,
Talk of rebellion for actions unkind
Serves as the watchword for those he has turned,
I may not have all but this have I learned.
Thou, my sweet Prince, art branded a coward,
80   For Phoebe's murder they lust to undo.
Whilst your Highness there is said deflowered
Then poisoned thy soon-to-be daughter through!
The Don did then whisp another fable
That ye tried to kill, but were unable,
The Queen! Of all preposterous fables
That one doth certain beat Kane and Abel's!
The fact that all were stowed in thy closet;
Phoebe all bloodied, stomach cramps was it?
And Jezebel stiffened, poisoned to death,
90   With thy Queen swooning and gasping for breath,
Did lend some weight to his mendacity,
Yet that he seeks is sheer audacity!
VALENTINO. 'Tis clear, my good soldier, we thank thee kind
And would have thee back, so we are not blind
To further facets of Grenaldo's plan.
OFFICER. Then I am gone to discern all I can.

49

VALENTINO. Pray thee, seek to uncover those other
Who are still safe to be labelled brother.
OFFICER. My Lord, I shall.

Exit Officer.

100   VALENTINO. See thee father, he would nothing fear now,
Has pushed fate further than we can allow.
What more passage to motivate action?
For pity's sake seek out satisfaction!
RUFUS. Sure reason thou comprise, 'tis utmost clear,
Evil's shadow wings immask o'er this land,
And though my heart doth break 'pon this I hear,
We now shall set to meet our final stand.
They may not find us too much in the sun,
But of a glory only blood can see,
110   For in the midnight mass of love undone,
That state of hate for us shall never be.
Ready thyself, take arms about thy waist,
Release thy servant, innocent I fear,
And make good show of him to all well-placed,
Yet keep thy guards about thee also near.
For seeing that his daughter's killer walks,
Parleys and beguiles, laughs then takes his ease,
I trust to stir the Don until he balks,
Chokes 'pon his pride, our will to thus appease.
120   Guided so within his foulest humour
Fortune's flare may hap to greet us kindly
By confirming true the oldest rumour:
The more foolish fool doth follow blindly.
Sharpen thy psyche for a thousand hits
And prepare thyself for this war of wits!

Enter Guard.

GUARD. My Lords, I bring a message from the Don,
He hath sent me to bid the King anon.

He stabs the King.

VALENTINO. Father!

Valentino stabs the Guard

Get thee to hell, thou desperate villain!

Valentino stabs him again.   *Exit Guard.*

130   VALENTINO. Father! Nay, yet stir thee not. O father!
RUFUS. O my Prince, I am weak and dying.
VALENTINO.   Nay, father.
RUFUS. Speak thee not, but hear me now. Take thee a wife,

As mine here ends, so begin another life.
Promise me, as I now upon thee die,
Thy ears shall hear thy new-born baby's cry.
VALENTINO. I thee promise.
RUFUS.   Avenge my death, O 'tis cold!
     He dies.
VALENTINO. Father! Nay, father? Peace be with thy soul.
     He kisses him.
O bloodiest vengeance, thou shalt be mine
And I'll govern thee as I marshal life!

140   All that would witness, bemark close this time,
To live, to die, to abide by the knife,
So tiny a thing, no more than this hand
Miss-used to take the most mightiest King!
Forgive me father, I late understand
The duty of bearing the royal ring.
A son I was not within thy short years,
That cuts me deeper than any blade could,
So swift to revenge, now barren of fears,
Redressing the poise as any man should

150   I shall resend the Don his own message,
Yet no errand-boy shall carry it forth,
But my hand alone will air the presage
To his most timely death. I swear henceforth,
As sure as the sun doth set in the skies,
So long as I still have blood in my veins,
These bitter-sweet tears that fall from mine eyes
Shall not, I avow, here cascade in vain.
I'll keep from the world thy painful passing,
As 'twould but serve to aid the enemies

160   Of peace, their armies now swift amassing,
Their sole purpose to bring love to its knees.
Rise then, dear father, we'll bear 'pon our back
And lay to rest afore we launch th'attack.
                       Exit Valentino bearing the King.

IV.2   *Enter Grenaldo, Isobel, and Maria.*
GRENALDO. Peace, Maria, and welcome to our home
That has by excellent exchanges grown
Wiser in its hosts, and that being so,
We offer tidings that all may now know
Our kind intentions, swift and sure to be
Uniting ourselves, ending enmity.

For none shall live that revere the opposed,
Our will is released, all secrets disclosed.
The King, as he was, did murder our girl,
10   Sweet daughter, kind Phoebe, hath left this world,
And this good Queen hath ta'en to her fortune
Our faction, which being most opportune,
Allows unto us certain rights of state;
Armourers, archers to stead-fix our fate.
Accepting that we can have but one King,
Rufus shall not live to see thy wedding
To his son, now beset by our sweet breath,
(Aside) I'll play along 'til I deal his death!
'Tis certain thou of the Prince wert smitten,
20   Even so much as once to have written
Verses of rhyme, in which there be no use,
But for those who needs must swift be seduced!
Yet, this is a sometime estimation
Perchance good time may voice consternation
For artisans and those who would practise,
Yet living without, 'tis sure that none would miss!
All being so, as 'tis as I have said,
Thou must be most pleased, the Prince to soon wed?
MARIA. I pray, where is your son, my Lord?
GRENALDO.   Abroad;
30   Hath sailed for England. So long he adored
To view that island, though I see not why,
The people are cold, the earth never dry!
The food is a famine, their empire's lost;
Joys of there living merit not the cost.
They do speak of one tiny oasis
Where kin are kind, I lose what the place is;
A port of some note, a famous abbey,
Daring sweet authors to on their wit be.
Nay, I have not the name about my tongue,
40   Alas, he is there, his song is here sung.
MARIA. Then happy am I to marry the Prince;
If it be thy will, I'll ne'er from it wince.
GRENALDO. Thou art as wise as seeming beautiful.
ISOBEL. She is, if not else, utmost dutiful.
Thanks good Maria, our soul is now calm;
To have such as thee upon our son's arm
Rekindles in us a sense of lost pride,

Yields a plentiful harvest inside
And for thy pains we offer great reward,
50   Now and forever for thee and thy Lord.
Joined as one that none shall put asunder,
Worthy successors to all hereunder:
Sapphires, gems, gold treasures and silver,
Minerals, charms, soft jewels and quicksilver,
Incenses brought from the earth's four corners,
Thickets and plants, local avifauna.
Heavenly kingdoms thou shall embody;
All shall be thine.
GRENALDO. *(Aside)* Over my dead body!
ISOBEL. All we solicit from thee in return
60   Is the sense of our son whose love has turned
Away from his mother in these late days;
Relight his dim heart and soul to our gaze.
'Suade him to marriage this midsummer's night
That all be settled as evening's light
Dips its fair wings upon the earth's shadow,
Soothing his wrath, like Jupiter's Juno.
MARIA. I shall in this and all other function
Follow thy command without compunction.
GRENALDO. Much thanks, kind Maria and so farewell,
70   Our guards shall aid thee divine where he dwell.
                    Exit Grenaldo and Isobel.
MARIA. So destiny swings itself about-face
Guiding my heart to its natural place
Beside and within Prince Valentino's,
So was it through-out, as surely he knows,
And yet I did not, there's a fierce passion!
To think we control ourselves is the fashion,
But I, like most, cannot harness my heart,
I have not the skill, the nature or art.
Forgive me, my love, for treachery's spent,
90   For malefactions which I here repent.
O how can a loving heart turn so sharp
To twisting the knife from playing the harp?
Our human nature is not so humane,
Such pits and falls would drive wisdom insane!
And like to myself, the Queen is now mad,
Confusing all sense, the good from the bad.
She has forsaken her own family,

Will have her poor husband trimmed from the tree
And all for the sake of cheap pride and lust;
100   As King, Don Grenaldo I'd never trust.
Murdered his daughter, Rufus of Florence?
I chance to find these lies an abhorrence.
That being so, I must to my lover
To speak my heart, without need of cover.
No longer to be fear's lost lonely slave,
For in wondrous wise kind love shall I rave!
So fail me not swift feet of fancy,
Fleet must we be to null necromancy!

Exit.

IV.3   *Enter Barthes.*

BARTHES. How now, sweet masters, pray forgive my frown,
Yet have I laboured hard and searched this town
And still no sign unearth I of the Prince,
From Phoebe's passing none have seen him since.
Not in the palace, mansions or hovels;
Nay, good Madame, I checked all the brothels!
It is as though he changéd into air,
Yet there's a thought to loosen out one's hair,
For 'tis said that those of true royal blood
10   Can magic themselves into mist or mud!
What then, should I crave to conjure the earth?
Have done, there's no loss in some playful mirth:
(To the earth) Sweet Prince, Valentino, be thee about?

Enter Valentino and Jacques behind.

VALENTINO. What ho there, Barthes, there's no need to shout!
BARTHES. *(Aside)* A miracle! 'Tis a miracle plain!
There's no pure logic or priest could explain!
Art thou well, my Lord, am I on thy face?
VALENTINO. What means thee, thou fool? Come hither, embrace!
BARTHES. Embrace thee, my Lord? I had rather not!
20   VALENTINO. Come pay me instant courtesy, thou clot!
BARTHES. Yet, my good Lord, I am well past thirty;
My knees are weak and the ground is dirty!
VALENTINO. Upon my life, such brazen disrespect!
Go to, you work for the Don I suspect?
BARTHES. Nay, nay, my Prince, my life is for the King;
For he and thee I would do anything!
VALENTINO. Then give me welcome as a servant ought,
With obsequious bending, not with sport!

BARTHES. Very well, my Liege, I shall then obey
30   And lie me down like a maid in the hay.
         He lies face down.
VALENTINO. What upon earth do you think you're doing?
BARTHES. Alas, 'tis 'pon the earth I am chewing!
VALENTINO. Good God! Of all the gooseberries I have seen,
Thou art by far away utmost supreme!
BARTHES. O thank you, your Highness, we aim to please.
JAQUES. For heaven's sake, Barthes, up on thy knees!
BARTHES. Jaques, my friend, he hath transformed thee too?
Be thee of the air or the earth anew?
JAQUES. I fear, my Lord, he hath lost his short mind.
40   Perchance he impaired 'pon some root unkind?
VALENTINO. 'Tis most certain he is out of his wit;
The dream hath turned real, his mind is split.
Come, let's aid the unfortunate fellow,
'Afore his manners migrate from mellow.
JAQUES. Thou art of late become most kind, my Lord,
And for my release forever adored.
VALENTINO. Enough, Jaques, thy durance was too long,
I should thee trust without purgation's song.
See thee Barthes, we stand at thy elbow?
50   How he doth start and his forehead furrow!
BARTHES. Great masters! I bow before thy power
And haste to tell ye at this late hour
To be on thy guard 'gainst Grenaldo's gourd,
Methinks for ye he plans actions abhorred.
For thy family too, the King, the Queen
And Jezebel face offences obscene!
Pray do not let him usurp thy city,
For with him it charge 'twould be so -
VALENTINO.   Pity,
Good friend, is a most excellent virtue
60   And we thank thee truly for what ye do.
BARTHES. Yet look to my mistress, I have but one,
I fear she hath lived too long in the sun.
Life's riches can oft true taste devour;
When savoured without the sweet is sour.
To not have felt the dream's pain and regret,
Is never to wake and happiness met.
JAQUES. Of what does he speak?
VALENTINO.   Grave dangers for all.

55

        Come, for Maria, we must not forestall.
Enter Maria with guards.
        Whither be thy mistress, Barthes?
        BARTHES.   Yonder.

70   JAQUES. *(Aside)* Why there's coincidence some would ponder.
        MARIA. Fair greetings, my Prince, I come as thy friend,
        Desperate with need of our mandate to mend.
        VALENTINO. Then wherefore approach with enemy guard?
        Unsheathe thee, Jaques. Barthes, *rest en guarde*!
        MARIA. Let us in private counsel each other;
        I have an offer from thy dear mother.
        VALENTINO. A little less dear since she served against
        Her husband and son, I have her dispensed.
        MARIA. Yet, hear me, my Lord, for the sake of peace.

80   VALENTINO. For thee I'll grant but the smallest release.
            They withdraw.
        MARIA. Too long now did I suffer and despise,
        Secretly bitterly 'gainst all thy sweet lies.
        In truth I passed that fine line to hatred
        And came to resent most all that ye said.
        Such powerful thoughts o'ercame my soft heart
        Encouraging me our ways to thus part
        By force, if my faithful love was not met,
        Alas now ashamed and full of regret
        I stand before thee and misdeeds confess,

90   Crimes that I now endeavour to redress.
        I with the Don plotted Jezebel's fall,
        Though I swear, 'pon my life, my part was small
        And, as it was, our gambit did fail
        Since Marcello was due to impale
        Thy bride, but strangely he did not make show,
        Leaving for England as far as I know.
        Thereafter, I admit, I was not sad
        To hear of Jezebel's passing, more glad,
        And headed in haste unto thy palace

100   Where my heart gave way to love from malice,
        For there thy mother did ask me to wed
        Unto her son, unto thee, and I said
        Aye, Madame, aye, and a thousand times aye!
        As something inside me broke with a sigh.
        I have done thee wrong with the thoughts I had,
        But trust me, my love, 'twas merely a fad!

And as thy love, I came hither to warn:
The Don has in store grave endings newborn.
He is determined to murder the king
110 Then, with thy death, will increase usurping
Until there be no worlds left to conquer,
Turning this place from city to bunker.
Have faith in me now when I tell thee true,
Thou art mine other, my all, I love you!
O, enough words! Let me on bended knee
Here ask of thy heart, wilt thou marry me?
VALENTINO. You yearn for yourself or my dear mother,
Or perhaps for her significant other?
The Don, I am sure, did himself order
120 This hasty show, to quell the disorder
Now running scared through his new harlot's mind,
I thank thee sincerely, nay, far too kind!
MARIA. Thou know'st, sweet Prince, I fend for myself.
VALENTINO. I know of nothing but revenge herself.
So much thanks for thy pains within thy speech,
My heart though, I fear, is well out of reach.
MARIA. As you wish, my Lord.
    Maria withdraws.
VALENTINO. Pray, when would they have this wondrous event?
MARIA. 'Pon midsummer's night, as light doth relent
130 Giving its way unto glorious dark.
VALENTINO. Perchance, for thee, there remains yet a spark
Of hope, of feeling, but no more than this:
Should thee expire, I would not long miss.
I'll consider thy offer as I must,
Without sweet emotion, devoid of trust.
So tell my dear mother and her new friend,
My mind they'll know with the morrow's moor end.
MARIA. My heart and soul shall then look to the sun
And pray with my life that God's will be done.
140 VALENTINO. Have peace! God has not the same will as man,
Do better and bend thy will to his plan.
Go, remember the King to my mother;
The past is a plague, as she'll discover.
                Exit Maria and Guards.
So Marcello was sent for my Jezebel?
Methinks he took Phoebe and his soul to hell!
And thus gives reason to his swift depart;

57

The Don hath cut his own son from his heart.
JAQUES. What news, my Lord, will justice be carried?
VALENTINO. Of sorts, Jaques, I am to be married!
    Jaques faints.
150 *(To Barthes)* Bring him, and I pray thee, do not snigger,
Foul and cunning plans must we configure.
                  Exeunt.

IV.4 *Enter Marcello, bloodied.*
MARCELLO. Sweet God o' mercy, say this be a dream!
Wake Marcello, let him live and be free
And find himself all wrapped in his bedding
As man or boy, he cares nought which it be!
'Tis there, we remember, a soft summer's day,
Innocent splendour as the sun's golden rays
Danced in the air, as did we 'bout the green;
Such peace, such love, so much yet unseen!
Say then I fell to a sleep with that night
10 And dreamt until now, perchance waking I might
See it is so, for it lingers in my mind;
I there see my sister, so happy, so kind.
Come then, foolish boy, here's not what it seems,
Calm thy hot senses, open eyes and see!
Yet, where is the world, the sun and the trees
And whither my sister? Still here upon me!
O lend back but a day, let time restart,
But a few poor hours to mend poor hearts!
Dear God, thou shalt, for sweet heaven ye must!
20 Wherefore, yet wherefore didst we father trust?
    He pulls out a dagger.
Marcello must so embrace suicide
For his too scolding sin, foul fratricide!
Farewell then false life, to hell with us now,
Perchance in the sequel we'll make ye proud.
O 'tis pitiful! A true father's son!
Such a cowardly act that saves no-one!
How brave Marcello! What selfish release!
Thy father's the cause, his effect must cease.
Aye, there's the root and shaft of all terror;
30 I'll yet serve my Lord and correct his error!
So be it, I swear, afore my soon death
To grace a son's ears with a father's last breath.
                  Exit.

V.1   *Enter Grenaldo, Isobel and Guard.*

GRENALDO. Confirm in thy speech, that staged in action,
So none may wrestle the crown from our grip.
Needs rest we safe in sure satisfaction,
Ne'er 'pon the three sister's humour to trip.
GUARD. I shall, my good Lord, attempt to disclose
The rumours finding themselves to mine ear.
All circumstance of the King's late depose
Note of his highness's fall into fear.
Once his most infamous metal did rust,
10   His heart did allow his nature to see.
Betrayal, incest, adultery, lust,
Disloyalty, murder, all within he!
So heavy, he lay himself 'pon his knife,
Too much in guilt, and betook his own life.
Leaving all unto his wife -
ISOBEL.   O husband!
GRENALDO. Weep not, gentle sister, for our brethren,
Let not the past gainsay thy future's course.
'Tis meet the King forewent himself heaven,
For of thy earthly hell, he was the source.
20   Thanks, my soldier, you may now take your leave;
Despite his actions, we must the King grieve.
                            Exit Guard.

Waste not thy tears lest upon two towers;
Thy husband fell as too did my child,
Yet I shall not wet the ground with showers
'Till midsummer's heat hath turnèd mild.
Not even this noon at her grave shall I,
Whilst shaking her ashes to heaven's disdain,
Loose but one tear for my heart from mine eye,
But steadfast power within shall remain.
30   Come midwinter's shrill shall we mourn those lost,
So enjoy thy treasure, then count the cost.
                            Exit Isobel.

Isobel, my love! My Queen! Isobel!
Enter Maria.

MARIA. Good morrow, Don Grenaldo.
GRENALDO.   What would ye?
MARIA. I bring good news of Lord Valentino.
Agrees he in kind, yet more in sorrow,
To venture under skies solferino

And pose his answer to our proposal,
Yet what that might be none on earth could glean.
GRENALDO. Saddened was he by the King's deposal?
40   MARIA. He spoke in a riddle, sans sense or mean,
Yet found I his portance assuring calm,
Much like your good self, yet lacking in charm.
GRENALDO. So be it, tonight ye shalt be married.
Assure the Prince our vengeance is carried
With his father's loss, there needs be no more;
Blood that has blood makes the bearer yet poor.
MARIA. I shall.
GRENALDO.   Come then, unto our daughter's grave,
Where men and the earth turn each other's slave.

                         Exit Grenaldo.

MARIA. So the King is lost and gone already?
50   When my sweet Prince strikes, I shall be ready.

                           Exit Maria.

V.2   *Enter Valentino, Jaques and Barthes dressed as a girl.*
BARTHES. Be thee certain, this is such a cute plan,
I've played many parts, but always a man!
VALENTINO. Trust me, good servant, this scheme has two prongs,
With which to be-fork our future along.
JAQUES. Explain me once more, O wise cunning Lord,
My role, as mistakes we cannot afford.
VALENTINO. O heavens to Betsy! Listen thee both:
The Don, we'll gouge, like a cancerous growth
From inside out, corroding his vessel,
10   His own shallow brain itself shall wrestle
When regards he Jaques, alive and free,
Playing the tabor and laughing with me.
The more we make jolly, the more he'll hate;
Desperate to kill thee, but he needs must wait,
For before our kin he can make no show
Of thy violent hungry death to know,
And for my mother, I shall play fancy
With thee Barthes; I'll be all romancy!
Long holding, soft kissing, sweet joy and mirth;
20   The more I love thee, the more shall give birth
New fears that I shall ne'er marry for love
Nor money, aye, she'll curse heaven above!
Blaming herself, her soul versus reason,
'Till all is clear, she staged her own treason.

Chance then within this new framework she'll turn
To our better trust, Grenaldo to spurn.
So upon this evening's ceremony
As the shadows grow, the light she may see.
Within that moment I shall assail
30   Grenaldo himself, his heart impale
Upon this dagger he sent my father,
Though by this arm I'll bury it farther.
When the hilt hath split his spinal column
There shall I twist, like a spade on solum.
But soft, but soft; aside. Here comes something.
        They move aside.
Enter Grenaldo, Isobel, Maria and Guards.
    GRENALDO. Blessèd father, take unto thy bosom
The soul of thy dear departed cousin,
Phoebe Grenaldo, who murdered to death,
We pray shall find peace with our heavy breath
40   Which shall for thee and her sing in prayer
As free as the guilty that live to dare
Cut short a pure life by vices impure,
In thy name, Lord, we'll not evil endure,
But strike back with force, an eye for an eye!
Our justice shall fall like rain from the sky,
For we be righteous in indignation!
So for God, for peace and for our nation
No expense of wealth nor human value
Shall be spared in the conflict we debut.
50   Ye took our daughter as sweet sacrifice,
To prove our love, for which there be no price
And so hath stirred our muscles to motion,
All debts shall settle through our devotion
To thy laws and prescripts, as thou hath set.
The perpetrators shall live to regret
The day that thou kindly granted them birth,
A father's revenge for a daughter's worth.
So as proud we are to serve thy good will,
We scatter her body to no more ill.
60   'Pon the wind then carry her soul to thee
There to relive, and exist happily.
      He scatters the ashes. Valentino comes forth.
VALENTINO. Bravo! Bravo! Did ye pen that yourself?
Look ye brethren, the new king is in health

And hath claimed himself as the voice of God
Here upon earth! What, will ye pilgrim plod?
You should, at least, have thy cute verse optioned
To be produced; such skill! Pure adoptioned
False piety, unspoken since Tartuffe
Spoke his blasphemous rhyme to raise the roof!
70   Come Jaques, let's praise the new messiah
With a humble ditty called *The Liar.*
Strike up brother and come skip my new love,
We shall sing and dance for Beelzebub!

       Jaques plays the tabor. Barthes dances.
VALENTINO. *(Sings) O The Liar he will trick thee,*
The Lair he will lie!
The Liar would convince thee
That the innocent must die!
With false words upon his mouth
And a hand upon his heart,
80   *The Liar will insist for peace*
Another war must start!
He'll murder his own brother
And then die within his wife!
The Liar has no concept
Of the worth of human life.
Yes The Liar he will trick thee,
The Lair he will lie!
The Liar would convince thee
That the innocent must die!
90   *In the name of God he'll slaughter*
In the name of God he'll kill!
In the name of God be careful -
Or he'll bring upon thee ill!
He'll feed upon thy deepest fears,
He'll call the truth a lie,
Be careful in the shower
If you ever question why!
For The Liar he will trick thee,
The Lair he will lie!
100   *The Liar would convince thee*
That the innocent must die!
Yes, The Liar he will trick thee,
The Lair he will lie!
The Liar would convince thee

That the innocent must die!
GRENALDO. He hath fallen into madness! 'Tis sad.
VALENTINO. If thy world be sane, we are haply mad.
Come hither, my love, ye dance like a queen,
Or much liken to one that once had been.
    He kisses Barthes.
110 Ah, what freedom to again play the fool!
How is't some prefer the devils' old tool
And haste into marriage? I see it not.
To bind for power is to lose the plot!
Go to, shall we venture unto the wood,
For the world needs think upon that they should.
JAQUES. Farewell!
BARTHES.   Goodbye!
VALENTINO.   *Auf Wiedersehen, adieu.*
'Till tonight at dusk, as the grass weeps dew.
               Exit Valentino, Jaques and Barthes.
GRENALDO. Doth he thee tickle, Lady Maria;
Something in thee his poor verse inspire?
120 MARIA. Nay, my Lord. 'Twas the lilt of lunacy;
I laugh to think that he sang it to thee!
GRENALDO. He hath defiled our daughter's demise
With his foolish jests, with insolent lies!
Hear, my Queen, this aggression will not stand!
We shall now, by force, take rule in this land.
Come!
               Exit Grenaldo and Isobel.
MARIA. *(Aside).* A song with Jaques, and Barthes dancing,
I near laughed so when I saw him prancing!
My lover is wise, I see his cool plan;
130 I shall from within augment all I can.
               Exit.

V.3 *Enter Guard.*
GUARD. Sweet Ladies and Gentlemen of Florence,
I bring ye news of good Friar Lawrence
Who travels this day to marry our Sire,
Prince Valentino with Lady Maria.
This happy event warrants thy presence,
Ye may bring donations, gifts and presents,
All shall be welcomed by our acting King
Grenaldo who, though grief stricken shall ring
The wedding bells in high praise and glory.

10 So we ask ye now to join our story
  As guests of honour awaiting the Prince,
  Eager to see what his feelings evince,
  Since rumour has it the Prince shall rebel,
  For he sees marriage as a living hell!
     Fanfare.

Enter Grenaldo, Isobel, Maria, Friar Lawrence, Marcello disguised,
Guards and Attendants.

  GRENALDO. Good citizens, welcome, all and sundry!
  To this celebrational panoply,
  Wherein we shall see our noble kin wed,
  Shortly followed by the crown 'pon our head;
  For we that have sat now long in mourning,
20 Sense a new era and time is dawning.
  So must we let go the follies of past,
  And build together a future to last.
  With these words I speak unto thy dear ears,
  I pray ye be moved, perhaps unto tears,
  And grace us with thy utmost attention
  Within this brief and happy detention.

Enter Valentino, Jaques, and Barthes.

  Yet here comes our groom, the Prince right on cue,
  So straight to church without further ado.
  FRIAR. Gathered are we within this holy place
30 To witness a Prince and Lady embrace,
  As a token of their love, two as one,
  For sweet souls that join may ne'er come undone.
  Assure ye then that this here be thy will,
  To marry together for good or ill.
  To cherish and love in sickness and health
  To prize above all, including thyself.
  Not to enshrine or on pedestal place,
  But to cherish with mind, body and grace
  Each other's beauty as much as thy faults,
40 Since nothing so grave more Heaven revolts
  Than mere attraction to splendour skin deep,
  Such false shallow sins the sewers shall reap.
  All questions thus answered within thy hearts
  We give thee a moment to speak or part.
  Lady Maria, do ye take this man
  To love and to honour as thy husband
  For nothing more than purest desire,

His life to enrich and to inspire?
MARIA. I do.
FRIAR.　　　Valentino, Prince of Florence,
50　In the name of God, I Friar Lawrence
Demand of ye to here answer in truth,
Wilt ye as a man of honour give proof
Of thy love and respect for Maria,
Do ye take this woman to admire,
To have and to treasure from this day forth,
By the prescripts of God always henceforth?
VALENTINO. I must confess, I was to say thee nay,
But something inside from her will not stray
Too far in my heart, for there she is Queen;
60　Though this notion to me had seemed obscene
I do, good Friar, take this sweet angel
As soley my wife.
FRIAR.　　　Come Heaven or hell?
VALENTINO. Push not this new spirit beyond it's means;
To bind is well, lest it well bind thy dreams!
FRIAR. By the power vested within my life,
I pronounce ye both as husband and wife!
　　　They kiss. Applause and cheering.
GRENALDO. Let us be the first to congratulate
And so hereby publicly reinstate
Our nephew, the Prince, as heir to the throne,
70　*(Aside)* Though with this poison his rise I'll postpone!
ISOBEL. O my sweet Prince hath made his mother proud!
VALENTINO. O my poor mother, still lost in her cloud!
ISOBEL. How now, my son, speak not in tongues of speed,
Thy father would be proud of this fair deed.
VALENTINO. A fair deed! Almost as fair, foul mother,
As kill a King, and marry his brother.
GRENALDO. Here, dear Prince, let us drink to thy union
A cup for thee and for our reunion.
VALENTINO. Much thanks, my King, uncle, Don Grenaldo,
80　Or perhaps my father, for who would know?
Yet set it by, I will drink it anon,
First I would have thy head crownéd upon.
GRENALDO. As you wish, my son, it shall then be so.
(Aside) There is yet some pride in Valentino.
Come ye courtiers and give thy trumpets sound,
This night shall in time befall most renowned

To all the world, for we here bury hate,
Symbolised henceforth, we shall rule this state.
      A fanfare.
Fair Valentino, ye shall crown the King,
90   And place upon our hand the royal ring.
         Guards bear the crown and ring. Valentino takes them.
VALENTINO. Let all then remember, I did here crown,
And set a royal sting within this clown!
         He draws and attacks Grenaldo. Marcello defends him.
MARCELLO. Peace, Valentino, this is not thy office!
VALENTINO. Why, Marcello, the true heir to the palace!
GRENALDO. Nay, my guards, let our loyal son defend;
'Gainst a soldier this Prince shall meet his end.
         They fight.
MARCELLO. I would not thee harm, but cannot permit,
Another's vengeance in my father sit.
VALENTINO. Then ye shall die, protecting the devil;
100   Come, try again, let us dance and revel!
         They fight. Valentino falls.
ISOBEL. O Marcello, I beg thee for his life!
GRENALDO. Run through him, my son, then covet his wife.
ISOBEL. Good Marcello, I here salute thy skill
And with this toast, pray do my son no ill.
GRENALDO. Nay, Isobel! I crave thee do not drink!
ISOBEL. For my son, I must. Wherefore do ye wink?
         She drinks.
There's for thee Marcello, now spare my Prince,
Yet what is this pain? Give us water to rinse
For our mouth is too dry. O Valentino!
GRENALDO. Look to the Queen.
110   VALENTINO.   Mother! O my mother!
ISOBEL. The drink! The drink! O my son, I here die!
         She dies.
VALENTINO. O villainy! Shall all blood-ties end with blood?
MARCELLO. They shall end, cousin, the son shall stem the flood.
         Marcello stabs the King.
ALL. O treason! Treason!
MARCELLO.   Aye, treason there is,
This is the King and the treason is his!
GRENALDO. His is mad! My guards, I am but wounded.
To hell with these traitors! Off with their heads!
         All fight.

MARCELLO. Hold! Hold all, I say! Part!
    All part.
Hear me those friends still loyal to the Don,
120 Thy senses have hither been played upon
For my father here did plot from the start
This kingdom and crown to usurp and part.
He ordered myself to kill Jezebel,
Which I swift carried out, yet could not tell
Betwixt Phoebe and the Prince's first bride,
With fate thus mocking I reaped fratricide
Upon my sibling, my sister, myself,
For a father's lust for power and wealth.
GRENALDO. This traitor lies! Denigration I say!
130 MARCELLO. Forgive me, father, unjust was thy way.
VALENTINO. Come then, uncle, let me join with thy son
And deliver this dagger.
    Valentino stabs the King.
GRENALDO.   O!
VALENTINO.   There, 'tis done!
Now for the twist I promised my father.
    He twists the knife.
GRENALDO. O!
VALENTINO.   There! Yet methinks it could go farther!
    He twists the knife again.
GRENALDO. O!
MARCELLO.   Goodnight, false king, may ye yet find peace
As thy son on earth grant thee thy release.
    Marcello cuts Grenaldo's throat. He dies.
Valentino, take up the royal ring.
All kneel before thee; long live the King!
ALL. *(Kneeling)* Long live the King! Long live the King!
140 VALENTINO. Much thanks, kind cousin, our first act shall be
To resolve this war, I thus pardon thee
And hereby create thee High Lord of Court,
Rise Don Marcello, from ill we shall wrought
A new kingdom, with thyself at our side.
Those who against us did plot shall be tried
And judged according to the law laid out.
Let none under-scale the weighty clout
That awaits them, for our rule shall be firm;
Never was there so much so quickly learned!
150 So now with our wife, fair Queen Maria,

We shall by instance nations inspire.
Our dominion upon such terms as these
We thus shall replant ourselves like the trees.
Tonight we'll bury our mother solemnly,
Sweet were too sour an epithet for she.
Our father, my King, shall be buried in state,
Henceafter thirty days mourning shall bate
Our universal breath in readiness
For a brave new world, ill-fate to redress.
160   Yet all misfortune is but a blessing,
Disguised so keeps the unfortunate guessing.
Thus I bow in respect of thy good will
And pray that some shall set paper to quill
And tell to thy daughters and sons to be
Of the ancient young Prince of Italy,
Who in but three days staged the strangest show,
From fool to a King; Prince Valentino.

He bows. Exeunt.

About the Author

Ryan J-W Smith was born in Dartford, England on July 7th 1974.

Following in the footsteps of great playwrights such as Oliver Goldsmith, J. M. Synge and Oscar Wilde he attended Trinity College, Dublin. Whilst at Trinity he wrote *Sweet Love Adieu* and was awarded the 'Hagan Dass Scholarship for Outstanding Achievement'.

The world premiere of *Sweet Love Adieu* took place in The Roman Theatre, St. Albans, England in July 2001.

Smith began writing his second verse play in New York; *The Power Play* was completed whilst living in Paris in March 2003.

Smith intends to continue writing plays in his unique style of verse.

www.ryanjwsmith.com

Glossary

Accord - agreement
Affray - frighten
Aloof - apart
Anon - soon, shortly
Approbation - approval
Averous *(coined)* greedy *(from Avarus)*
Avifauna - birds
Barren - infertile
Beget - produce
Beguiles – charm deceptively
Behest - command
Bemark - mark
Bemock - mock
Bene nox – good night
Benet - catch
Beset - ready
Beteem - allow
Betook - took
Betroth – engage to be married
Betwixt - between
Breaches - breaks
Brethren - brother
Caveat Emptor- buyer beware
Censure - judgement
Chyme – acidic fluid
Cipher - nothing
Compunction – scruple
Con - know
Concord - harmony
Consternation - anxiety
Contrite – remorseful
Cur - dog
Cuttle - knife
Deem - consider
Denigration – unfair criticism
Depose - testimony
Derogate – deviate from
Diapause – suspended development
Dribbling - Failings
Drudge - labour
Durance – imprisonment

Duteous - dutiful
Enmity - hostilities
Enrapture – pleasure greatly
Epithet – characteristic adjective
Ere - before (in time)
Ergo - therefore
Feckless - irresponsible
Fleet - nimble
Fordone - exhausted
Forestall - prevent
Forewent - preceded
Gainsay - forbid
Gambit - trickery
Glissades - slides
Gourd – false dice
Had as lief – should like as much
Henceafter -from then
Hither - to this place
Hoe - whore
I'fecks - in faith
Imbrue - shed blood
Immask – Cover, hide
Importune - inconvenience
Indignus! – unworthy!
Jarp - smash
Jocund - cheerful
Juno - Roman goddess
Lackey - manservant
Lascivious - lustful
Malefactions - crimes
Metal - spirit
Mete - aim
Misconster - misconstrue
Nefarious - evil
Nonpareil - unequalled
Obsequious - obedient
Panolply – splendid display
Parleys - talks
Perchance - perhaps
Perfidious - deceitful
Perforce - forcibly

Ponder - consider
Portance - behaviour
Prat - beat about the arse
Prendo una donna! - I pick up women!
Presage - omen
Prurience - wantonness
Purgation - purification
Rend - give
Rudesby - insolent person
Sanctum - private place
Sconce - head
Scupper - thwart
Shrift - confession
Smitten - obsessed
Smite - strike
Solferino – reddish-purple colour
Sooth - truth
Solum - upper layer of soil
Stratagem – strategy
Strumpet - prostitute
Transpierce - pierce through
Unfetter - disturb
Venture - dare, dare to go
Wanton - unrestrained
Whence - from what place
Wherefore - why, for what
Whither - to what place
Whoremonger - lecher
Whoreson - son of a wore
Withal - with it, besides
Withstand - oppose
Zion - heaven

Some commonly used verbs in archaic 2nd person

Canst - can/could
Didst - did
Dost - do
Hadst - had
Hast - has
Hath - *(3rd person)* has
Mayst - may
Mightst - might
Shalt - shall
Wast - were
Wert - were
Wouldst - would

Common Contractions

Is't - is it
Ne'er - never
'Tis - it is
'Twas - it was
'Twere - it were
'Twill - it will

2nd Person Archaic Pronouns

Thee - *(singular, subjective case)* you
Thou - *(singular, objective case)* you
Ye - *(plural)* you
Thy - your
Thine - yours

Available from the same author:

Sweet Love Adieu

"Imagine Romeo and Juliet. Now add Manuel and Basil from 'Fawlty Towers'. Next put Mercutio in a dress and give Juliet a moustache. Sprinkle in a pinch of sex-starved, drug-making Friar. Add a little thigh-slapping, sword fighting and thumb biting. Mix it all up with half a dozen Shakespearean devices, write the whole thing in iambic verse, place your tongue firmly in your cheek and enjoy!"

The Dream Theatre Company

"...the most original comedy of errors since Shakespeare's own."

"It takes a brave man to take on Shakespeare at his own game, but Sweet Love Adieu – essentially a distillation of Twelfth Night and Romeo and Juliet – succeeds thanks to its sizzling comic energy..."

"His sweetly romantic play cracks along at a good pace with a fine script..."

"...the dialogue is extremely adept with some very funny couplets peppering the script along with some great audience asides."

"...highly accomplished...this play's a comic delight."

"There *is* culture – if you want it"

Observer Newspapers

"It's staggering! It really is staggering! Brilliant! I love it!"

Steve Le Fevre, BBC Radio Leeds

"...an inspirational playwright."

JVC

A romantic comedy in five acts

ISBN 0-9515956-2-8